Also by Frederic Schuler

FLAMEWORKING

Glassforming

BY FREDERIC AND LILLI SCHULER

CHILTON BOOK COMPANY PHILADELPHIA
NEW YORK
LONDON

Glassforming

GLASSMAKING FOR THE CRAFTSMAN

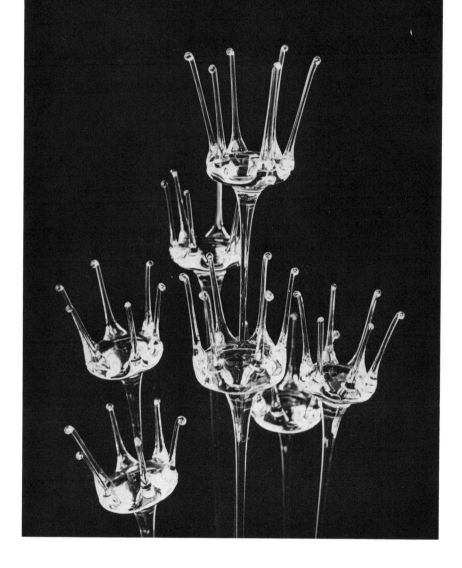

Copyright © 1970 by Frederic and Lilli Schuler
First Edition
All rights reserved
Published in Philadelphia by Chilton Book Company
and simultaneously in Ontario, Canada,
by Thomas Nelson & Sons, Ltd.
ISBN 0-8019-5558-0
Library of Congress Catalog Card Number 71-135056
Designed by William E. Lickfield
Manufactured in the United States of America
by Radnor Graphic Arts and
Haddon Craftsmen

We dedicate this book to Christopher Merret, physician, chemist, botanist, member of the Royal Society of England, and translator of Antonio Neri's *L'Arte Vetraria* (*The Art of Glass*), 1612.

Merret's *The Art of Glass* was published in 1662. It went beyond a simple translation of Neri's text, which was devoted primarily to the chemistry of glassmaking, to include Merret's own commentary or "Observations" on the construction of glassmaking furnaces and on tools and techniques then used in England. The translation and commentary had much more impact on the glass industry than did Neri's work, for it was Merret's work which was translated into German, French, and Spanish, with various editions—even as late as 1776.

In this second book on glassmaking, we hope to continue to advance the primary goal of Merret, namely:

"To the ingenuous Reader," to bring together all that is known about glass, its manufacture and use.

Preface

As Administrator of Scientific Research for the Corning Museum of Glass from 1956 to 1958, I have had the unique opportunity of observing glassblowers at work and of talking and working with Frederick Carder, founder of the Steuben Glass Works. When I met Mr. Carder he was ninety-three years old, keen and alert, and going to his workshop each weekday. There he experimented with the duplication of diatreta vases, using casting techniques. With his help and advice I studied the duplication of shallow bowls from the Alexandrian-Roman period using fusing and casting methods. Mr. Carder was an important influence in strengthening my interest in glass-making techniques. He had a very extensive knowledge of glassmaking, having invented, rediscovered or explored practically every technique associated with blowing. My contact with the Corning Museum of Glass and all its artistic activities strengthened my general interest in glass and the crafts.

Then for a number of years I did little work in glass except for continuing some studies on ancient techniques. Instead, I concentrated on drawing and sculpture in clay and plaster. In early 1967 I again started to work in glass. I used a direct method—flameworking—which I had enjoyed very much previously. This proved to be exciting, especially after my wife started to work with me and we saw the rapid evolution of our designs. Such a design evolution is a grand experience that can be the good fortune of all who choose to work in this field, for there are many unexplored ideas and objectives. With our renewed interest, it seemed only natural to resume work in other glassforming techniques, particularly casting, which offered new design possibilities. Here, too, rapid design evolution has proved exciting.

I wish to thank Paul Perrot, Director of the Corning Museum of Glass, for his aid with photographs from the museum collection and Stanley Weisenfeld, Supervisor of Media, Corning Glass Works, for his help with photographs for this book. When I worked for the Corning Museum of Glass, Mr. Weisenfeld helped with photographic projects which gave me greater insights into techniques.

For this book, James Chen of Santa Barbara helped with photographs of our glass and of techniques. I was very pleased to work with him.

I wish to thank Ruth Hurst, Assistant Curator, Pilkington Glass Museum, Lancashire, England, for her assistance with photographs of models and exhibits.

I also wish to thank Robert W. Brown, of Glendale, California, who for ten years has been doing exciting things in glass, for photographs of his work and for pleasant visits to his studio.

Frederic Schuler

Santa Barbara

My interest in glassmaking started when my husband joined the research laboratory of the Corning Glass Works in 1953 and worked on photosensitive glass. That glass had architectural and design applications which I found interesting. I followed the progress of his scientific work there, visited the Steuben Glass factory often to watch the glassblowers and the engravers, and saw his ideas on ancient techniques evolve when he worked for the Corning Museum of Glass. I also enjoyed meeting Frederick Carder. My husband and I talked about setting up a workshop on our farm near Corning and we got as far as looking at some pottery workshops near Alfred, New York, and making some sketches for our place.

After we moved to Santa Barbara I helped Fred with his studies on ancient casting techniques. I had a chance to learn more about moldmaking from a delightful Italian, Federico Quinterno, then eighty years old. When my husband started to work again with flameworking techniques, I started experimenting with my own designs and methods, and this work has continued. Together we have seen rapid changes in our designs. We had talked often about the artistic and decorative potential of other methods of forming glass—in particular, casting—and we decided to work with these methods rather than just talk about them.

Lilli Schuler

Contents

Part Two | Forming Techniques

Part Three | Forming Equipment

Part Four | Design

Part Five | The Story of the Glassformer's Material

Appendices

Glassforming

Part One | Introduction

1. THE UNIQUENESS OF GLASS

*f*Glass is a unique and exciting material. Of all the glassmaking and glass-forming techniques available to the craftsman, the direct techniques of flame-working and glassblowing prove to be the most dramatic in execution. These direct methods capture the imagination of the person fascinated by skill and manual dexterity. As the surfaces produced are very smooth, the methods lead to objects which have a special aliveness in their transparency, colors, and optical imaging effects (see Figures 1 and 2). There can be dynamic and changing patterns when viewed under various lighting conditions. The results can likewise capture the imagination of a person interested in design.

There are other, indirect methods, in which the glassforming technique is not particularly dramatic, but the result is as exciting as any produced by flameworking or glassblowing. Further, the resulting object could not have been produced by direct methods. Large panels—rectangular, circular, or any outline—vibrant with color under transmitted light, can be produced by sagging, laminating, and enameling in combination. Such panels resemble a painting, and an artist interested in color and pictorial or abstract design may easily become absorbed by the potential of glass (see Figure 3). Shapes that are sculptural in form, with sharp edges and textured surfaces, can be produced by casting methods (see Figures 4 and 5), and in addition they may have transparency and color. Artists interested in shapes and forms may easily become fascinated by glass.

The uniqueness of glass depends in part upon its physical properties. For example, casting and fusing certainly emphasize the metal-like properties of glass. Today we talk about the fluid properties and the viscosity of glass,

1

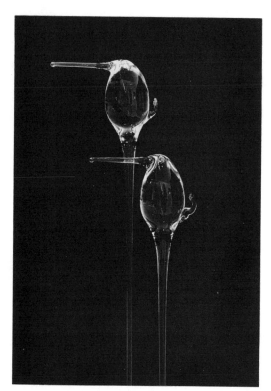

Figure 1. "Hummingbirds."

Figure 2. "Puffins."

Figure 3. *Decorative panel by Robert W. Brown.*

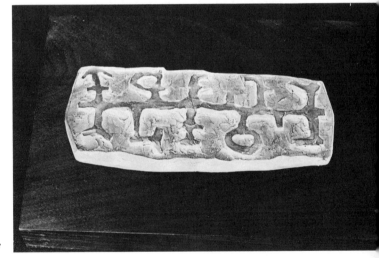

Figure 4. "Monogram."

Figure 5. "Maze."

but in the seventeenth century glass was referred to as a "Metall" when in the molten state:

> "The Servitor, when the Metall is sufficiently refined, puts his hollow Iron into the pot, and turning it about, takes out enough for the vessel or work it is intended for, the Metall sticks to the Iron. . . ."
>
> *Christopher Merret, in the commentary to his translation of Antonio Neri's* The Art of Glass, 1662

This is an interesting description, and when considering some of the methods discussed in this book, one perhaps should think of glass as a "transparent metal." The object produced, whether panel, shallow bowl, relief, vase or sculpture, may have the heavily textured surface of a metal casting. In addition, the advantage of transparency and vibrant color, with visible interior or rear textured surface, offers design possibilities. There may be complementary designs on two surfaces, a situation unique to glass or other transparent media. Obviously, with lighting from the front or rear, different effects may be achieved in a single piece.

In general, the surface texture of a work in glass may be further enhanced by grinding and polishing, using lapidary techniques. The work could be made from a massive piece of glass, as was done by Erwin Burger for his "Fox" (see Figure 6), or the piece could have been preshaped by casting techniques and finished, in a simpler manner, by lapidary methods. One can roughen the surface of very smooth blown glass, smooth and polish the surface of slightly matte cast glass, do subtle diamond-point engraving, or do copper-wheel engraving. Some of these methods have been adapted to work on flat panels and could be combined with laminating and enameling techniques. Modifications of copper-wheel engraving, using flexible-shaft rotating grinding wheels, permit work on very large panels. Examples are the work by John Hutton (see Figures 7 and 8). These panels are two of a series. Mr. Hutton has many fine panels in the Coventry Cathedral.

We shall find out that glassmaking has a wide variety of interesting techniques. Some are unique to glassmaking, like sagging, laminating, flameworking, and glassblowing. Others, like lapidary grinding, enameling, and casting are adapted from other crafts.

This book will concentrate on those glassforming methods which involve heating and softening of the glass, but will exclude flameworking and glassblowing. Thus it will include sagging, laminating, enameling, fusing, and casting.

Figure 6. Detail of "Fox" by Erwin Burger.
(Corning Museum of Glass)

Figure 7. "Brigantia" by
John Hutton.

Figure 8. "Coventina" by
John Hutton.

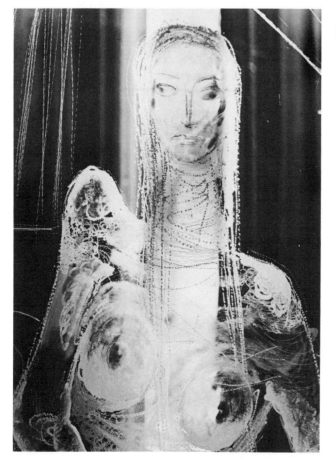

2. TECHNIQUES FOR THE INDIVIDUAL

Focus on the Individual

We wish to concentrate on techniques that a craftsman can use when working alone. Most of the art glass produced today in a glass factory is the result of a team approach. The glass designer makes sketches and drawings, and the glassblowing team, called a "shop," executes the piece. It would seem reasonable to assume that in the Ancient Period and the Alexandrian-Roman Period (see Section 3 below) an individual craftsman could have both designed and executed glass bowls and other shapes. Therefore we must turn to some of the ancient methods to look for technique simplicity.

Glassmaking is at an exciting stage today, with emphasis shifting from the team to the individual. The craftsman or art student in college or high school learns to work alone using the techniques of flameworking, casting, fusing, sagging, laminating, enameling and even glassblowing (called "free-blowing" also) if the latter is modified properly.

Flameworking is of interest because it is exciting, direct, and the least expensive glassworking technique. With it, one can produce marvelously shaped forms, simple or intricate, working with glass rod (see Figures 9 and 10). If one works with tubing and blows, then hollow vaselike sculptures can be made (see Figures 11 and 12). These may be combined with wood or metal. The technique has been described in a previous book: *Flameworking* (Chilton Book Company, Philadelphia, 1968). The technique of flameworking, or reheating glass rod or tubing or other pieces of glass, is also called "lampworking." This method was used at least as early at 1660 to shape microscope lenses; the simple burners were derived from small oil lamps.

With this technique, the glass is heated in only that area where the piece is to be sealed, enlarged, or changed in some manner. The cool ends of the glass are held in the hands, which control the rotation and position of the fluid central portion. Today the scientific and commercial applications require handling large and heavy pieces of glass and fabricating very complex shapes. To meet these needs, glassblowing lathes have been developed which permit all of the flameworking operations to be performed under mechanical control. Excellent examples of such work are the helium and hydrogen cryostat (see Figure 13) and the equilibrium still (see Figure 14) made by the James F. Scanlon Co. It is important to realize that one can do marvelous designs without a lathe and using a small, inexpensive burner.

Glassblowing—that is, free-blowing or offhand blowing—is more difficult than flameworking and requires more elaborate and expensive facilities. This is an ancient technique, for the blowpipe was invented around 50

7

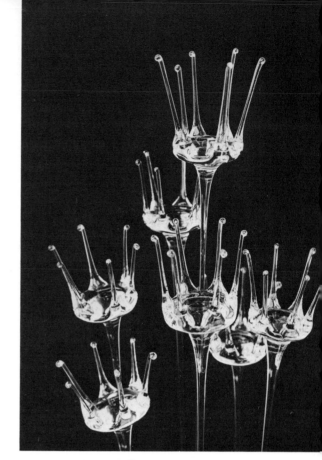

Figure 10. *"Asters."*

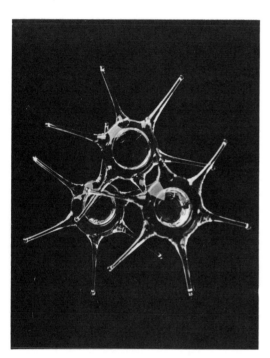

Figure 9. *"Daisies."*

Figure 11. *Bubble sculpture.*

Figure 12. Hexi-bubble sculpture.

Figure 14. Equilibrium still by
James F. Scanlon Co.

Figure 13. Helium cryostat
by James F. Scanlon Co.

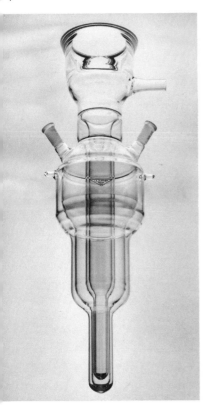

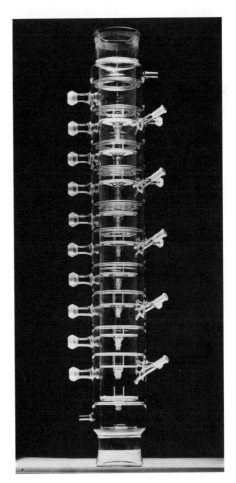

B.C. Blowing developed into a group or team effort. Glassmaking techniques were well developed by 50 B.C., as glassmaking was already 1500 years old at that time.

For blowing, glass is manipulated and shaped at the end of a hollow iron pipe (the blowpipe or blowiron), which is about four feet long. Molten glass from the furnace is wound or "gathered" on the top of the pipe. It is then shaped and inflated, tooled, sheared, and spun out or forced in (see Figures 15 through 17). More glass can be applied and decorated by various operations. The shape at the end of the iron is maintained at the proper degree of fluidity by reheating periodically in a small furnace called the "glory hole" or reheating furnace. Great skill and coordination are required to gather, to shape and to keep the glass under control on the iron. There has been a revival of interest in the handicraft aspect of glassblowing, with quite a few universities or colleges setting up facilities and offering courses. Their approach has been to revise and simplify procedures so that a person may work alone.

There are other techniques which are part of the contemporary excitement about glass, especially as they can be executed by a person working alone. They are: casting, fusing, sagging, laminating, and enameling. These techniques open up different approaches and offer perhaps even greater opportunities than do flameworking and glassblowing (free-blowing). They do not involve the coordination and manual dexterity of the latter two techniques, and from that point of view may be considered much simpler. Individuals with limited manual dexterity can design and execute pieces which are indistinguishable from those of a person with greater dexterity, or which could be compared with those done by glassblowing. Moreover, the design potential is so great, involving large, freestanding colored windows (especially simple with the use of epoxies), rough textures, variations in thickness, sharp edges, and complex hollow regions, that these techniques could be considered more advanced or refined artistically. The techniques of sagging, laminating, and enameling resemble painting, while the techniques of fusing and casting resemble sculpture. Typically, one would work from sketches and cartoons, or from models. In casting, the model would be precisely replicated in glass.

Casting and fusing are ancient methods. The early work, which is quite remarkable, must have been done with the simplest of furnaces and techniques. This should offer encouragement to the beginner—with the technical knowledge available to him surely he can do work as fine as that done by one of Tutankhamen's craftsmen! Modern technical knowledge offers many opportunities—one can break away from the traditional leaded technique of stained-glass windows and mount the glass with epoxies, using a collage or "hard-edge" technique. One can enumerate other advantages—the steel wheel cutter is a great advance over the hardened steel point of the twelfth century, when Theophilus described glassmaking.

10

Figure 15. Gathering glass.

Figure 16. Marvering glass.

Figure 17.
Measuring a spun-out disk.

The Workshop Layout

Our own glass shop is small and unsatisfactory in many ways, but since we are privileged to live in a mild climate, we do most of our messy work outside. However, if we could plan a workshop from the beginning, we would try to consider all aspects of the glasswork to be done. Here are suggested areas to be considered:

1. *Space for Drawing and Modeling*

   Space is required for drawing and modeling. Small drawings can be made at a desk; large drawings require a large surface for full-size execution. Work in clay, plasticine, and wax requires separate space for each.

2. *Main Workshop*

   The main workshop should be laid out to handle whatever kind of glasswork is planned. It should have a good work-flow pattern, wall space to mount drawings, good ventilation and heating, adequate space for glass storage and glass cutting, and work space for glass layout and assembly. Whenever its use is possible, equipment on wheels may save much physical effort.

3. *Space for Glazing*

   Separate space for working with glass colors and enamels is desirable but not necessary. That will depend to a great extent on designs and methods of working.

4. *Area for Working in Plaster*

   Water is needed to work in plaster. Maybe you will want to do your work in clay here too. Plaster, clay, and molds will have to be stored. The old molds will be broken up here. This is going to be an unavoidably messy area.

5. *Space for Furnace*

   The furnace should be readily accessible so that it will be easy to move glass from the main workshop and from the glazing area to the furnace. Molds also must be moved to and from the furnace.

6. *Space for Acid Etching*

   The acid-etching area should be separate and well ventilated to avoid fumes and corrosion problems.

12

7. *Business Office Nook*

It is important to keep adequate business records, work and experimental records, and to have a place for reference books.

8. *Packing Space*

Space is required to lay out the glass to be shipped and to store packing materials for glass, which tend to be bulky. Plastic bubble pack, for instance, comes in rolls of 3-foot diameter.

The equipment within each of these areas will be discussed in the different sections on glassforming and testing of glass. There is a very good discussion of the equipment for stained-glass work, and also of the studio layout, in Patrick Reyntien's book, *The Technique of Stained Glass* (Watson-Guptill Publications, New York, 1967.)

3: A BRIEF HISTORY OF GLASSFORMING TECHNIQUES

INTRODUCTION

The history of glassmaking is interesting because of the variety of techniques which can be adapted to meet our needs and because of the mystery associated with them. Glassmakers have been secretive, or at least uncommunicative. They obviously derived some of their techniques from other crafts but also made original inventions which remained unique to glassmaking because glass has unique properties. The methods have had interesting cycles of growth and decline; certain methods remain a mystery—we see the results, can even duplicate the object, but we are by no means certain that our method is the same as the ancient one. Our emphasis is not on the detailed history of glass objects and techniques, a history that is not very clear in many respects. We would rather stress the simplicity of early techniques that are of interest to the craftsman working as an individual rather than a team member.

CASTING AND FUSING TECHNIQUES

The Ancient Period

The Ancient Period is a long introductory period from the fifteenth century B.C. to the third century B.C. which brought forth hollow-glass techniques[1]* and the casting of figurines and statuettes, and later shallow bowls[2] in Egypt, Mesopotamia, and Syria. The earliest hollow ware makes its appearance about 1500 B.C., while the earliest datable glass sculpture comes somewhat later during the reign of Amenhotep II (1436–1411 B.C.). The actual origin of glass is of greater antiquity and certainly must have evolved out of the use of glazes for ceramics. It is thought that the Egyptians were the first developers of glass as a decorative material, although it is possible that the North Syrians preceded them.

The early technique for hollow ware involved what is known as the "core" method. There is no descriptive ancient literature on the method; excavations have produced finished objects rather than partially finished ones, so they give no clues as to the method. However, the early craftsmen obviously did use a core, and the objects were not blown or inflated. I have duplicated the basic shape, using a casting technique around a core, followed by "fire-polishing."[3] Dominick Labino has demonstrated that the basic shape can be manufactured by trailing glass onto a heated core.[4] Whatever the technique, it must have been quite simple, and with it marvelous flasks and vases were made (see Figures 18 through 20), though limited in design.

* See Appendix 3 for numbered references in text.

14

Figure 18. Egyptian core vessel (Corning Museum of Glass).

Figure 19. Egyptian core vessel. (Corning Museum of Glass).

Figure 20. Egyptian core vessel. (Corning Museum of Glass).

The Egyptian glass industry declined around the tenth century B.C., only to recover somewhat later, though the later core vessels did not match the earlier ones in quality.

"Shawabtis," or mummiform figurines, were made by casting methods. These figurines were intended to represent servants in the next world. The casting methods surely evolved from metal casting. Statuettes of persons, royal heads, and heads of horses as well as parts to complete a sculpture, like eye linings, were all cast (see Figures 21 through 24). At a later date, certainly by the seventh century B.C., hemispherical bowls of almost transparent clear glass were being made by some kind of casting method (see Figures 25 and 26). I have studied such bowls and duplicated them by casting.[5]

Finally, it should be mentioned that glassmaking became more widespread in the Ancient Period. Finds of glass outside of Egypt are not always in the Egyptian style and that suggests the spread of the manufacturing. Further, the techniques of cutting stones were adapted to glass, so that some glass is decorated with carved hieroglyphs or cartouches.

The Alexandrian-Roman Period

This period from the second century B.C. to the first century A.D. was one of dramatic changes in the history of glass manufacture. The city of Alexandria became a preeminent glass center, though the lack of glass finds or glass factory excavations in Alexandria makes it by no means certain that glass was actually manufactured there. Rome might well have been a major center of manufacture. One can observe from the objects of this period that four methods were certainly in use: casting, mold-fusing, mosaic, and blowing, with the possibility of a fifth method that lies between mold-fusing and blowing.

Casting of clear hemispherical bowls continued into this period, along with other shapes, like boat-shaped saucers, which were finished by lapidary methods. Mold-fusing stands as a separate technique. It was an adaptation of casting, and involved an assembly of bits of patterned glass in a mold, followed by fusing.[6] Each piece of glass was considerably distorted, but the overall pattern was distinctly related to the original design (see Figures 27 and 28).

Much more remarkable is the technique used for the manufacture of miniature mosaics, first made around 300 B.C. The more elaborate ones are marvelously detailed (see Figures 29 through 31). These mosaics were used alone, or apparently assembled into larger mosaics, or used as decorative elements in the mold-fusing method described above. These mosaics are so small and have such detail that they obviously involve a procedure which started with a larger design followed by a "reduction in size" step—that is, a heating and stretching procedure. I have considered such methods[7] but the

16

Figure 21. Egyptian cast statuette.
(Corning Museum of Glass).

Figure 22. Egyptian cast relief head.
(Corning Museum of Glass).

Figure 23. Egyptian cast
or fused relief head.
(Corning Museum of Glass)

Figure 24. Egyptian cast eye lining.
(Corning Museum of Glass).

Figure 25. Ancient cast bowl. (Corning Museum of Glass).

Figure 26. Ancient cast bowl.
(Corning Museum of Glass).

18

Figure 27. Mold-fused bowl. (Corning Museum of Glass)`

Figure 28. Mold-fused bowl. (Corning Museum of Glass)

details are by no means certain. The technique a present remains an intriguing mystery. If a mosaic-glass factory should ever be excavated, there is hope that finds of partially completed mosaics will reveal the details of the technique.

Blowing, the most important technique for the history of glassmaking, was invented during this period. When one studies the history of invention closely, one discovers that there is seldom a dramatic birth of an invention—rather there are precursors which lead to it stepwise. This may be the case also for blowing. Consider objects like those in Figures 32 and 33. They are truly little masterpieces, with green, blue, white, purple, and clear bands, and with gold foil in the center of the clear band. This patterned glass would have involved, in Alexandrian times, assembly by some mold-fusing technique. The hollow shape with twisted and stretched pattern and "shattered" gold foil suggests an inflation or blowing step. I have suggested[7] that these shapes could have been mold-fused into a shallow bowl and then picked up out of the mold on an iron rod (which would have the role of the pontil or punty iron of today), shaped by reheating and tooling into a bowl, and finally forced almost closed so that a blowiron could be attached and the object finished with blowing techniques.

If the above is correct, true blowing (which would involve the steps of gathering molten glass from the furnace and then shaping it on a flat surface, followed by inflation) could have been an evolutionary process rather than a dramatic invention. The invention of blowing in the complete sense, including gathering, is thought to have taken place around 50 B.C. There is no direct literary evidence, although Gaius Plinius Secundus, or Pliny the Elder (A.D. 23–79), confirms that date in a negative sense. That is to say, he does mention inflation, but not the introduction or invention of blowing, in his few comments on glassmaking. It seems reasonable to suppose that if the invention had taken place during his own lifetime, he would have pointed that out; his failure to do so suggests that it was already a well-known and accepted technique. Further, blown objects are dated by archaeological techniques to the first century B.C., so that the above date is reasonable.

With the rise of free-blowing, which produced shapes like those of Figures 34 and 35, and of mold-blowing, which must have followed almost immediately and produced hollow ware like that of Figure 36, the other techniques soon fell into disuse. The production of objects was multiplied manifold, and casting and mold-fusion were displaced and forgotten.

Domination by Blowing

For our knowledge of techniques over this long period of time from the first century A.D. to the 20th century we depend not only on glass finds but also on written texts, at least for the second half of the period. For example,

20

Figure 29. Miniature fused
mosaic, length 2.8 cm. (1.09 in.).
(Corning Museum of Glass)

Figure 30. Miniature fused
mosaic, length 3.3 cm. (1.29 in.).
(Corning Museum of Glass)

Figure 31. Miniature fused
mosaic, length 3.2 cm. (1.25 in.).
(Corning Museum of Glass)

Figure 32. Gold-band glass flask.
(Corning Museum of Glass)

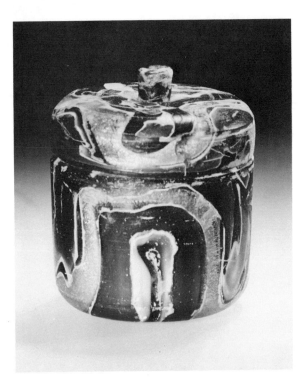

Figure 33. Gold-band pyxis.
(Corning Museum of Glass)

Figure 34. *Free-blown glass.*
(Corning Museum of Glass)

Figure 35. *Free-blown glass.*
(Corning Museum of Glass)

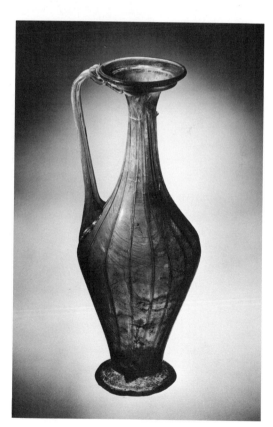

Figure 36. *Mold-blown glass.*
(Corning Museum of Glass)

two texts discuss blowing techniques: Theophilus Rugerus, *The Various Arts* (translated by C.R. Dodwell, London; Thomas Nelson and Sons, Ltd., 1961), of about 1110-1140 (the dates are not known precisely); and Agricola, *De Re Metallica*, 1556 (translated by H. C. Hoover and L. H. Hoover, 1912; Dover Publications, 1950). Later comes Merret's work of 1662, previously referred to. There is no mention of casting methods; fusion of bits of patterned glass and the making of the miniature mosaics are long since forgotten. Thus if casting methods were used they undoubtedly had very special purposes, possibly to furnish glass for the trade as a raw material.

A mysterious example of a casting almost too fantastic to imagine is the huge piece of glass found at Beth She'arim, near modern Haifa. The slab was manufactured in a cave near Beth She'arim between the beginning of the fourth century and the end of the seventh. It measures 11 feet by 6½ feet and is estimated to weigh almost nine tons. It must have been made in its own furnace and then the furnace dismantled after cooling. Such a piece is obviously one of those at present unexplainable and exciting exceptions.

The Rediscovery of Casting

Of course, pieces of glass were cast during the eighteenth and nineteenth centuries; after all, large pieces were required for lenses and mirrors of telescopes. But during those periods there does not seem to have been any casting done for artistic purposes. Then Decorchemont started working with glass using a casting technique—first around 1904 with an opaque glass, but by 1920 with transparent colored glasses. Some of his objects appear translucent because of the slightly matte surface. He executed massive bowls and vases, some boldly faceted, others with simple, powerful designs in bas-relief (see Figure 37). Obviously, they were not made by ladling glass, but by mold-casting—the heating of mold and glass together—for the delicate mixing of colors can come about only from starting with bits of colored glass. (The Corning Museum of Glass has other examples of Decorchemont's work.)

The Work of Frederick Carder

In 1904, Frederick Carder, then 40, came to America from England and founded the Steuben Glass Works in Corning, New York. This company was taken over by the Corning Glass Works in 1918 and Mr. Carder became art director for the entire Corning Glass Works. In the 1920s and 1930s Mr. Carder designed much of the architectural glass which was produced in quantity by the Corning Glass Works. He specialized in casting large reliefs, like murals for Rockefeller Center. Some of these were made by ladling molten glass into a preheated mold. Following his retirement in 1934, Mr. Carder continued to experiment with casting techniques in a studio in the old Steuben plant, working quite actively even up to 1960. During that period he

Figure 37. Cast bowl by Decorchemont.
(Corning Museum of Glass)

modeled in clay or wax, and cast the glass, using a wide variety of subject matter (see Figures 38 and 39), including carved filigree-style objects and diatreta bowls.

Technical Achievements

There are industrial examples of casting and fusing large pieces of glass. The Corning Glass Works was asked in the fall of 1931 to try to cast the famous Mount Palomar 200-inch reflecting telescope disk, using its low-expansion borosilicate glass. Dr. George V. McCauley, a physicist in the research laboratory, was put in charge of making the disk. A ribbed-back design for the disk was chosen to give greatest strength for the least weight. To provide the ribs, the mold had ceramic cores. The mold was inside an igloo-shaped oven made from heat-insulating bricks. This oven was heated by gas burners to keep the glass fluid during the six hours required to transfer glass by ladles from a 64-ton mass-production melting tank. Each ladle held 400 pounds of glass.

In March, 1934, the first 200-inch disk was made after experiments on 30-inch, 60-inch, and finally 120-inch disks were completed. Some of the cores broke loose when metal tie rods inside them melted. This first disk was used for test purposes and is now in The Corning Museum of Glass. After some redesign of the mold, the second disk was cast in December, 1934. In six hours, two crews of men poured 42,000 pounds of molten glass into the mold, using three ladles running from the continuous tank on overhead trolleys to the three pouring doors of the casting oven. The mold was on an elevator platform which lowered it from the casting oven into a basement. There it was moved on rails to an electrically heated annealing oven. In that oven it was held at constant temperature for two months, then cooled gradually for eight months by dropping the temperature seven tenths of a degree centigrade each day. Finally, in March, 1936, it was shipped to Pasadena for grinding and polishing.

The Corning Glass Works in 1967 made two large fused-silica (glassy silica rather than crystalline silica) mirror blanks, one 157 inches in diameter and 25 inches thick, the other 144 inches in diameter and 20 inches thick. The first blank weighed about 18 tons; the second, about 12¾ tons. They were made from smaller pieces of glassy silica, carefully preshaped by grinding, arranged in a pattern and fused together. Glassy silica was used for the mirror blanks because of its very low coefficient of expansion, its thermal stability, hardness, mechanical strength, and finishing properties.

The 144-inch piece was fabricated from seventy-eight pieces of glassy silica. Before fusion, there were six layers, with seven hexagonal components and six triangular components per layer; after fusion it was a monolithic disk (see Figure 40). The material is transparent and thus can be examined for internal flaws before grinding and polishing.

Figure 38. Cast glass by
Frederick Carder.
(Corning Museum of Glass)

Figure 39. Cast glass by Frederick Carder. (Corning Museum of Glass)

Figure 40. Fused telescope mirror blank, Corning Glass Works.

Enameling (and Staining) Techniques

The Ancient Period

Although there are some examples of enameling or fired painting on glass in the New Kingdom, there are more examples from the Alexandrian Period. Considering the relative scarcity of fragments, this technique was apparently not so important as the more direct decorating techniques at that time.

Roman Through Medieval, Including Islamic

In the period of the second to the fourth century A.D., glass painting continued with high skill and there were combinations of gilt and color. This kind of work was undoubtedly done in all the important glass centers—from Antioch to the Rhineland. Although some painting and gilding continued, there was a general technical decline after the fourth century (until the twelfth century).

After the seventh century, Islamic glassmakers made contributions in surface decoration. In the twelfth century or earlier, they decorated by chromatic surface techniques using simple designs. There was a burst of activity in the thirteenth and fourteenth centuries involving elaborate enameled and gilded mosque lamps. Luster stains on both exterior and interior surfaces of vessels evolved during this period, starting perhaps as early as the eighth century. Many of the vessels and lamps now in possession of European cathedrals or museums were brought back by returning Crusaders.

Several different shapes were used for forms on which to apply the decoration, but the mosque lamp has survived in greatest numbers. These lamps were designed to be hung from the ceilings of mosques by chains attached to the handles. They were made for the Mameluke sultans and their emirs. They frequently bear the name or personal symbol of the donor along with an inscription from the Koran (see Figures 41 through 43).

Theophilus Rugerus, who was mentioned earlier, proves to be a source rich in description of such processes in his sections on working both glass and metal. The decoration on glass is for church windows and includes, in Part II, chapters of his *Various Arts* titled:

> XIX—The Colour with Which the Glass is Painted
> XX—Three Shades of Colour for Highlights in the Glass
> XXI—The Embellishment of a Painting on Glass
> XXII—The Kiln in Which the Glass is Fired
> XXIII—How Glass is Fired

And in Part III:

> LIV—The Enamel
> LV—Polishing the Enamel

29

Anyone interested in or curious about the history of techniques will find these sections, and others, very interesting.

Theophilus does not describe any specific windows, but talks only in a general manner. However, Abbot Suger, who was responsible for the construction of the Abbey Church of St. Denis (1144), did describe some of the windows, in particular "The Tree of Jesse" window. This is one of the earliest known church windows, and it and others are described in the abbot's *On the Abbey Church of St. Denis and its Art Treasures* (Erwin Panofsky, Princeton, 1946).

The use of staining and painting for church windows continues from the twelfth century until today, and church windows really are the major artistic direction of the technique. The technical problems of working with flat glass are extreme, so that laminating and enameling are impossible for large areas.

Renaissance

Enameling became important in Venice in the second half of the fifteenth century. Glassmakers had been brought to Venice from Constantinople toward the middle of the eleventh century to produce mosaics for the Basilica of San Marco. By the thirteenth century the Venetian glassmaking industry was well established, and in 1291 was moved to the nearby island of Murano because of the fire hazard. The first enamel patterns used color and gilt in jewel-like patterns. Then, in the first half of the sixteenth century, German coats of arms were applied, for sale in the north. Later in that century, German craftsman began to enamel their own relatively crude glasses with coats of arms. The technique became very exacting and dominated production of decorated glass during the sixteenth and seventeenth centuries, although engraving became important after 1650 (Figures 44 through 47).

A rococo style was developed in the eighteenth century, using light translucent washes of enamel with greater freedom and rhythm involving a variety of subjects—portraits for example.

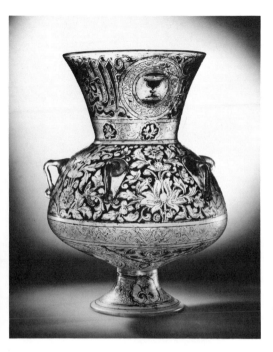

Figure 41. *Islamic enameled mosque lamp.* (Corning Museum of Glass)

Figure 42. Close-up of lamp in figure 41. (Corning Museum of Glass)

Figure 43. *Islamic enameled mosque lamp.* (Corning Museum of Glass)

Figure 44. Venetian enameled goblet.
(Corning Museum of Glass)

Figure 45. Venetian enameled goblet.
(Corning Museum of Glass)

Figure 46. Venetian enameled goblet.
(Corning Museum of Glass)

Figure 47. Venetian enameled goblet.
(Corning Museum of Glass)

Modern

Commercial mass-produced examples of enameling are ever-present, from labeled bottles to decorated drinking glasses. An artist can hardly compete with the commercial silk-screen processes, and even if doing a higher quality type design, he will probably use silk-screen techniques himself. The examples (Figures 48 through 51) show current craftwork, which one recognizes can be taken over by a factory and produced on a larger scale.

The more interesting types of craftwork today involve the full range of techniques, including lamination, colored glass, enamels, trapped air, and colors in the interior, with a great enrichment of color and design and a close analogy to painting (see Color Plates 1 through 4).

Figure 48. Vase by Frantisek Tejml.
(Glass 1959, Corning Museum of Glass)

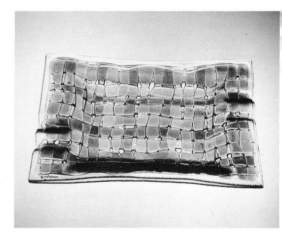

Figure 49. Ashtray designed by
Francis and Michael Higgins.
(Glass 1959, Corning Museum of Glass)

Figure 50. Plate by Maurice Heaton. (Glass 1959,
Corning Museum of Glass)

Figure 51. Four trays designed by Eugene M. Winters.
(Glass 1959, Corning Museum of Glass)

4. PHYSICAL PROPERTIES OF GLASS

There are several physical properties of glass which are important for the glassforming techniques of this book. We can use the picturesque language of Christopher Merret of the seventeenth century:

> "But to shorten this comparison, I shall here set down the properties
> of glass . . .
> > 'Tis artificial.
> > It melts in a strong fire.
> > When melted 'tis tenacious and sticks together.
> > 'Tis friable when cold, which makes our proverb,
> > As brittle as glass."
>
> *Antonio Neri*, The Art of Glass, *1612,*
> *translated by Christopher Merret in 1662*

Or we can stress, in more modern language, that glass has the properties of a *solid* at low temperatures and the properties of a *liquid* at elevated temperatures. There is a transformation between these two properties, not at some sharp melting point temperature, as with most materials, but over a range of temperatures. By rapid cooling, a fluid or distorting shape can be "frozen-in" (see Figure 52). Finally, the property of being *transparent* is important, with the possibility that the glass can be transparent-clear, transparent-colored, or semitransparent-opalescent.

The *solid* property that is most important is the "thermal expansion" or expansion-with-temperature relation. This is the property that complicates sealing different glasses together. It is a property of glass and other rigid materials—metals for example. A piece simply changes length with temperature, expanding a very small amount as the temperature is raised, and contracting or shortening as the temperature is lowered. Thus two different glass compositions will usually have their respective expansion-temperature relations differing just as with two different metals. If two thin strips of glass of different composition are sealed together side by side, upon cooling one will contract more than the other, and the strip will bend. This bending is like that of bimetallic strips used in thermostat controls. Because glass is brittle, the strip may fracture from stress if the length difference is excessive. In laminating and fusing different glasses together, or in enameling or casting with glass mixtures, a typical failure is due to this expansion "mismatch," commonly referred to as "incompatibility."

These expansions, or contractions, are small. A typical soda-lime glass rod, which is considered to be a "high expansion" glass, if 10 cm. (3.9 in.) long, will expand only .027 cm. (.01 in.) on being heated from 0°C to 300°C

36

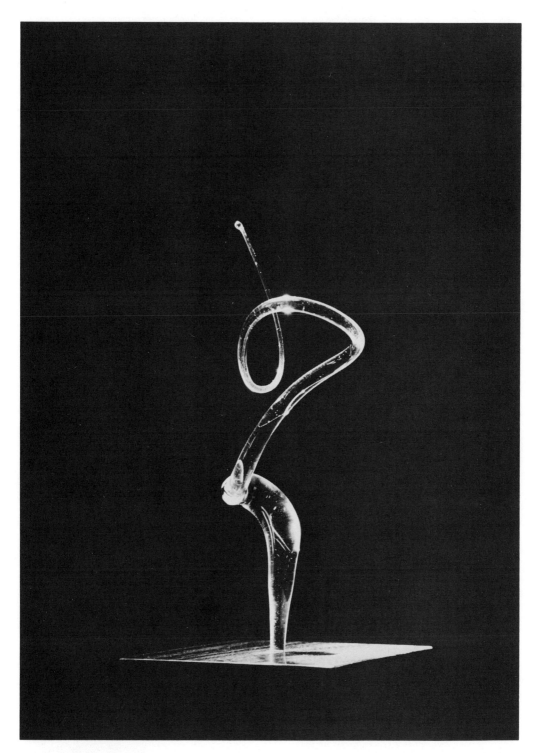

Figure 52. *"The Bo Tree."*

(32°F to 572°F). This thermal-expansion property requires the testing of all glass being used when different glasses or different colors are being sealed together. (The expansion property, the testing procedure, and other physical properties are described in greater detail in Appendix 1).

The *liquid* properties are important for casting, fusing, laminating, sagging, and enameling. As a molasses like or taffy like liquid, glass will slowly flow down and fill a container, or mold, with a horizontal free surface. A free surface will tend to round over from a surface-tension effect so small bits end up like flattened ellipsoids. Further, two glasses will "wet" each other and seal together.

When glass is cast, the process takes longer than the casting of much more fluid metals, and mold and glass are kept hot until the glass has flowed down to fill the mold. In a shallow relief mold, the free upper surface will be horizontal, except for the outer edge. Details of the mold will be replicated just as in metal casting, provided a sufficiently high temperature like 1000°C, is attained so that the glass is fairly fluid.

To the contrary, in sagging and laminating, the glass deforms at a lower temperature so that it is not very fluid, and the surface in contact with the mold will remain relatively unmarred. In enameling, the glass enamels soften much more than the base glass and will wet and seal to it. These properties will be illustrated in the discussions of techniques and explained in greater detail in Appendix 1.

Work with specific commercial glasses will also be described there.

Part Two | *Forming Techniques*

5. FORMING BY SAGGING AND LAMINATING

INTRODUCTION

Sagging or bending of glass has been used both commercially and by craftsmen for many years. An example is given in Theophilus's book *The Various Arts*. He describes the process for opening a blown cylinder, to make flat window glass, in Chapter IX: "Spreading the Sheet Glass" (in Book II). The cylinder has been cracked or "split" down one side and placed in a furnace:

> "When it begins to get soft, take some iron tongs and a smooth piece of wood and, opening it up in the part where the split is, you spread it and flatten it out with your tongs according to how you want it."

Here, of course, the bending process involves the active manipulation of the glass by the worker. The so-called "cylinder" process of making flat glass was being used in the nineteenth century on a large scale. As with Theophilus, a cracked cylinder was heated in a flattening furnace. The crack ran the length of the cylinder, and with crack uppermost, the cylinder simply unrolled in both directions outward from the crack. Without the crack, the glass would have softened and collapsed. The cylinder process was superseded by sheet-drawing processes. Increased demands for bent glass evolved out of the automotive styling changes, with the introduction of curved windshields and rear windows starting about 1932.

Before one can sag or laminate glass, one must first cut it to a desired shape. With the development of such a skill, one can consider a modern

39

offshoot of stained-glass windows; namely, assembling cut flat glass with epoxy cements. Very exciting windows can be made without the conventional "leads," which are a restricting design element.

Sagged glass, without enamels for decoration, is very limited in design potential. But if one uses epoxies, then curved strips, deformed bottles, and other glass can be assembled into a more complex decorative sculpture.

By laminating different colors, along with sagging, either a stained-glass window or a decorative sculpture can be made. It is, of course, fused into a single piece of glass. It is here that the technical difficulties occur, for the same thermal-expansion property and similar softening behavior are required in the elements to be assembled. Glasses from different manufacturers, or even different glasses from the same manufacturer, usually have different properties. Colorants added to a base clear glass will change the properties, but most manufacturers have no need to readjust physical properties, because they do not intend to seal glasses together. In laminating, if some compromise is made, with part of the work bonded with epoxies, a wider range of colors can be easily obtained. Fifty years ago such a technique did not exist, although some cements for optical elements were quite permanent. A person like Frederick Carder would have worked hard to adjust his compositions to "match," while today with good epoxies one can bypass the chemical composition difficulties and consider only the design aspects.

The process of forming glass by sagging can be divided into four steps: making the molds, preparing and cutting the glass, sagging or bending, and annealing. In Section 6, on glass colors and glass enamels, the decorating of the glass is added after the second step, with the other steps remaining the same.

Mold Materials

Our first choice for sagging glass is a permanent mold of red terra-cotta. This mold can be used for hundreds of firings. It is made with conventional clay-shaping techniques, fairly thin (¾″) to avoid warping when drying and firing. It can be made over some kind of form if desired.

The second choice is a commercial plaster mixture, Hydroperm, a product of the United States Gypsum Company. It is a plaster with some refractory material mixed in. This mixture is worked exactly like plaster, so it can be used to cast against a clay shape, or can be worked directly while still plastic. It has low firing shrinkage, but if there is any tendency to crack, then 200 mesh silica can be added to the mixture to reduce the firing shrinkage and therefore reduce cracking. It is still quite strong after firing and therefore can be used quite a few times.

The third choice is another commercial plaster, Hydrocal, also a product of the United States Gypsum Company. To reduce firing shrinkage and cracking, two parts of 200 mesh silica to one part Hydrocal should be used. This mold, after firing, is moderately strong. Casting plaster can be used in place of the Hydrocal, and that will decrease the cost.

FORMING THE MOLDS

The molds are made using conventional plaster-forming techniques. This is discussed in detail in Section 8 under "Forming the Molds."

SELECTION OF THE GLASS

Almost any kind of flat glass can be used for sagging or bending. Obviously, one would not start with laminated safety glass, or window glass with wire embedded in it, or tempered glass. If one starts with a reasonable choice, then the condition to be met would be avoidance of surface haze. That is, after firing the surface should not have changed appearance (see below in this section: "Devitrification of Glass"). Sheet glass from the Blenko Glass Company, Inc., from the Kokomo Opalescent Glass Company, Inc., and from the Paul Wissmach Glass Company, Inc., should all prove adequate, although we have tested only the first two. Commercial window glass shows some surface hazing if overfired.

A flat glass sheet of the above glasses, including window glass, can be used for enameling. Here, the proper glass color or enamel with respect to coefficient of expansion (see Appendix 1) must be selected. Most of the companies which manufacture glass colors indicate that they have compositions which are suitable for the different glasses.

Lamination of glasses is more difficult. For the different-colored glasses to seal together properly they must have similar softening behavior and matching thermal expansion properties; i.e., be "compatible." The glass should be at least 3-16" thick, and can either be smooth or have a textured surface. One should not mix glasses from different manufacturers. There are even some doubts as to whether all glasses from a given manufacturer are compatible. Brochures and current price lists are available from the manufacturer, and samples must be obtained for testing before you order in quantity.

The suppliers are listed in Appendix 4. The glass is made in the United States or Europe by the methods described in Part five, Section 21. The glass should be tested, cut to shape, sanded along the edges, carefully cleaned, and then, with the mold, placed in the furnace for firing. These steps will be discussed in detail below.

TESTING THE GLASS

At this stage we are concerned with only two tests or observations: sagging and its relationship to type of glass, shape of piece, and temperature; and laminating, or sealing, and its relationship to type of glass, shape of piece, and

41

temperature. By type of glass, we mean composition, for the composition affects the way in which the glass softens as the temperature is increased. This is discussed in detail in Appendix 1, "Physical Properties of Glass." By shape of glass, we mean the dimensions of the piece.

Let us consider sagging first. Some of the effects of shape or dimensions of the piece can be illustrated by considering the sagging of a bar of glass supported at the ends. It is rather obvious that at an elevated temperature a long bar of a given glass will sag faster than a short bar of the same glass.

One can make specific tests on bars of glass. To prepare a test bar from sheet glass, cut strips of uniform width using the wheel cutter. Measure the width, b (see Figure 53), the thickness or height, h, the length or span, L, and the weight, W. Mount on ceramic supports at each end so the bar can sag when heated. Heat in the furnace to a sagging temperature (650° C), hold for a few minutes' time, $\triangle t$, and then cool. Measure the sag, $\triangle y$, in the center, in centimeters.

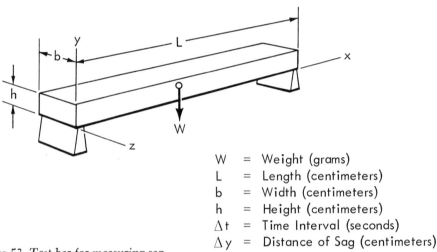

W = Weight (grams)
L = Length (centimeters)
b = Width (centimeters)
h = Height (centimeters)
$\triangle t$ = Time Interval (seconds)
$\triangle y$ = Distance of Sag (centimeters)

Figure 53. *Test bar for measuring sag.*

Not only does the length affect how a given bar, supported only at the ends, sags at a fixed elevated temperature, but the weight, the thickness, and width also have their effects. The thinner the bar the faster it will sag.

There is a fundamental sagging equation:

$$\text{Sagging Rate in Center} = R = \frac{\triangle y}{\triangle t} = K \; \frac{WL^3}{bh^3}$$

$$\text{Distance of Sag in Center} = \triangle y = R \cdot \triangle t$$

Here, "k" is a "materials constant"—it depends on the composition and therefore varies from glass to glass at a given temperature. It is not really a constant for a single composition but varies with temperature. That is, it depends on the viscous properties of the glass, which in turn depend on the

42

temperature. This equation will be discussed further in Appendix 1, and the nature of the "k" developed.

In this equation the length enters as the third power or cube—it has a pronounced effect on the sagging rate; likewise the thickness (height) enters into the equation as the inverse third power—it also has a pronounced effect on the sagging rate.

Suppose we start with a rod of "standard" dimensions as a basic reference. We then compare with it thicker glass, glass with a greater length, glass with a greater width, and glass that is loaded with a weight. We can then build up a table (see Table 1).

TABLE 1:   SAGGING RATE OF GLASS

	DIMENSIONS				
	Reference Bar	Double Length Bar	Double Width Bar	Double Thickness Bar	Double Weight Bar
Length	L	2L	L	L	L
Width	b	b	2b	b	b
Height	h	h	h	2h	h
Weight	w	2w	2w	2w	w
Load on Bar	0	0	0	0	w

From the above, and by use of the equation $R = K \dfrac{WL^3}{bh^3}$:

Sagging Rate	R	16R	R	¼R	2R

We can observe the following from the table, or we could set up the equivalent experiment:

> Bars with longer unsupported span sag appreciably faster than shorter bars.
> Thicker bars sag more slowly than thin bars.
> Increasing the width of narrow bars has no effect on sag.
> Increasing the weight (loading a bar with additional weight) increases rate of sag.
> Doubling the time at sagging temperatures doubles the amount of sag for a given bar.

All of these effects are "dimension effects." The "temperature effect" for a given bar is that as the temperature is increased the bar sags faster. The quantitative study of this effect is considered in the appendix. One can ap-

43

proach it qualitatively, studying the sagging of a set of identical bars at 650°C, 700°C, and 750°C, for example. You will discover then that the rate at 700°C is about ten times as fast as the rate at 650°C, and that the rate at 750°C is about 100 times as fast as that at 650°C.

As for the sealing of identical glasses, separate experiments can be conducted to check sealing temperatures. Sealing will require contact and therefore depends on sagging if the pieces do not have good contact initially. The sealing temperatures are in the deformation temperature range (Appendix 1).

Sealing together different compositions having different physical properties is a complex subject. There is a simple test to verify if the thermal expansion properties match. This test is described in the appendix, but briefly it involves cutting two thin strips, sealing them together using the flame of a burner (a flameworking burner or even a small propane torch) and pulling out a fiber which will have the glasses side by side. If this fiber does not bend upon cooling, then the glasses have matching thermal expansion properties.

Cutting the Glass

The simple operation of cutting the glass is the key operation to carry out any given design. It is of such importance that it should be described in detail to cover straight cuts, curves, ovals, etc. The workshop revolves about two centers—the layout and glass-cutting center, and the furnace. One needs an adequate work bench with free space around it so that there is easy access. There must be tabletop space for drawings and cartoons, as well as space for cutting and handling large sheets of glass.

For cutting, a smooth, firm but resilient surface is required—an old rug or a blanket stretched over wood. The following notes will aid you in the cutting procedures. They are presented in a condensed outline form, and some of the statements will be immediately obvious, once you begin to think about cutting glass.

Tools
    Steel (or tungsten carbide) wheel cutter
        Use as the basic tool.
        Break in a new cutter—make twenty long scribe marks.
        Use newer cutter for thin glass.
        Use older cutter for thick glass.
        Dip into turpentine or 3-in-1 machine oil—a definite procedure for breaking off narrow ⅜" strips.
        Use notches on cutter for breaking off narrow slices—use like pliers.
        Fletcher wheel cutter is recommended.
    Glazier's diamond point
        Use as a special tool—good for very thin glass.
        Use when precision is not required, as the diamond point cannot be seen—it is hidden by the tip.

Figure 54. *"Eastern" grip for cutting glass.*   Figure 55. *"Western" grip for cutting glass.*

Wooden straight edge
    Use wood, not steel—metal moves against metal.
Plastic curved templates
Circle cutting machine
Oval cutting machine

Holding the Glass Cutter
    "Eastern" grip—pull (see Figure 54)
        Hold cutter by thumb and fingers, with ball of cutter between
            first and second finger.
        Hold cutter perpendicular to scribe mark but tilting toward you,
            in direction of pull.
    "Western" grip—push (see Figure 55)
        Hold cutter by thumb and fingers, with ball of cutter resting against
            the inside of the hand, as if holding a pencil.
        Hold cutter perpendicular to scribe mark, as with "eastern" grip,
            but tilting toward you, against the direction of push.

Scribing the Glass for Straight Breaks
    Pull or push relatively slowly and smoothly—cutter wheel "sings."
    Make a light cut (heavy cut has much "hackle").
    Make one scribe mark only.
    Attempt to break—if scribe mark too light, make new mark 1/32" away
        from old—never go over old cut.
    Avoid running cutter in scribe mark, or dropping, as wheel will be
        damaged—damaged cutter sounds wrong (throw away).
    Cross a cut at about right angles.
    Continue a cut by sliding cutter gently into end of scribe mark and
        then start.

Breaking the Glass

Break the glass immediately—glass gets "stale" and the cut reseals itself.

Use tapping technique—tap reverse surface by putting scribe mark down; short scribe mark, one tap in center; long scribe mark, tap at end to start and lead crack by tapping just behind the tip of the crack.

Or, use pressure (bending) technique—scribe mark up, lay glass over a pencil aligned with the scribe mark, and press glass on both sides of the mark with palms of hands, until glass breaks.

Or, use finger-bend-and-pull technique—scribe mark up, thumbs top side, first fingers below and folded so that first joint supports the glass, thumbs and first joints close to the scribe mark; bend and pull apart with even and equal action; bend down to open crack and pull apart to have the crack propagate along the scribe mark.

Or, use pliers technique—scribe mark up and tip of pliers right up to the edge of the scribe mark with pliers on one side and fingers on the other; bend down and pull away at the same time; pliers is first choice for the beginner when possible to use.

Scribing the Glass for Curves

Push cutter for scribing the curve.

Use additional scribe marks to break out glass which is binding because of the shape of the curve.

Designing the Pattern for Simple Curves

Scribe simple curve, tap back to crack and break off—scribe additional marks only if necessary (see Figures 56 and 57).

Designing the Pattern for Complex Curves

Scribe, tap back to crack, break off; when glass binds or is likely to bind, use additional scribe marks; tap back to crack, break pieces off in order (see Figures 58 and 59).

Designing the Pattern for Circles or Ovals

Scribe, tap back to crack, break out; glass is almost certain to bind, so use additional scribe marks; tap back to crack, break pieces off in order (see Figures 60 and 61).

Cleaning Up

Keep bench free of glass splinters so that sheets lie flat when cutting.

HEATING CYCLES: GLASS SHAPE, THICKNESS, AND COMPOSITION

The sagging process is straightforward—at elevated temperatures glass softens and deforms under the action of gravity. Firing the kiln for glass is like firing it for pottery. With glass there is only one firing and the firing cycle would be like that for a bisque firing, but shorter than the ceramic cycle.

Either an electric kiln or a gas-fired kiln may be used. The heating can be done as rapidly as possible consistent with not breaking the glass by "heat shock"; firing slowly and cautiously does no harm. A typical cycle, which

Color Plate 1. "Sun-God" by Robert W. Brown.

Color Plate 2. Panel by Robert W. Brown.

Color Plate 3.
Panel by Robert W. Brown.

Color Plate 4.
Crest by Robert W. Brown.

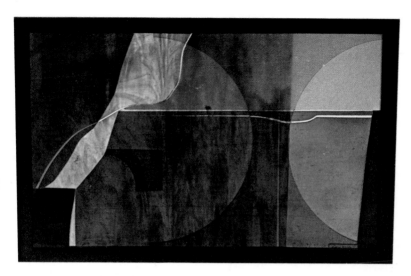

Color Plate 5. Panel by Robert W. Brown.

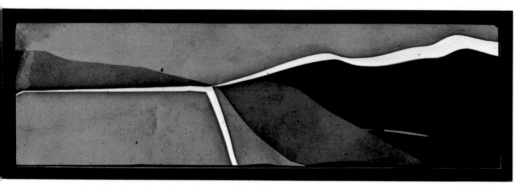

Color Plate 6. Panel by Robert W. Brown.

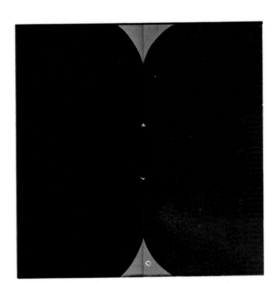

Color Plate 7.
Panel detail by Robert W. Brown.

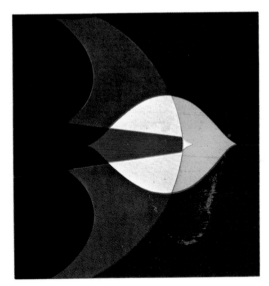

Color Plate 8.
Panel detail by Robert W. Brown.

Color Plate 9.
Sculpture by Robert W. Brown.

Color Plate 10.
lpture detail by Robert W. Brown.

Color Plate 11.
Tribe of Benjamin.

Color Plate 12. Detail of Tribe of Benjamin.

Color Plate 13. Tribe of Issachar

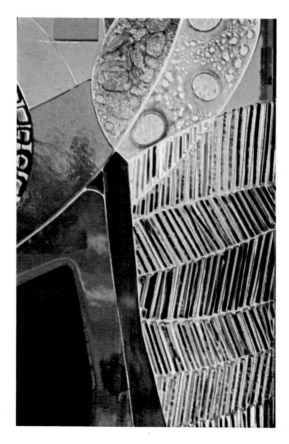

Color Plate 14.
Detail of Tribe of Issachar.

Color Plate 15.
Tribe of Levi.

Color Plate 16. Detail of Tribe of Levi.

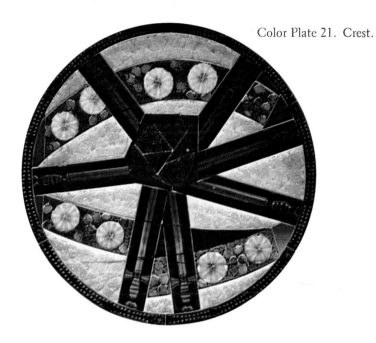

Color Plate 21. Crest.

Color Plate 22.
Detail of crest.

Color Plate 23. Relief.

Color Plate 24. "Sun-Burst."

Color Plate 25. "Mountains of the Moon."

Color Plate 26. "Fish."

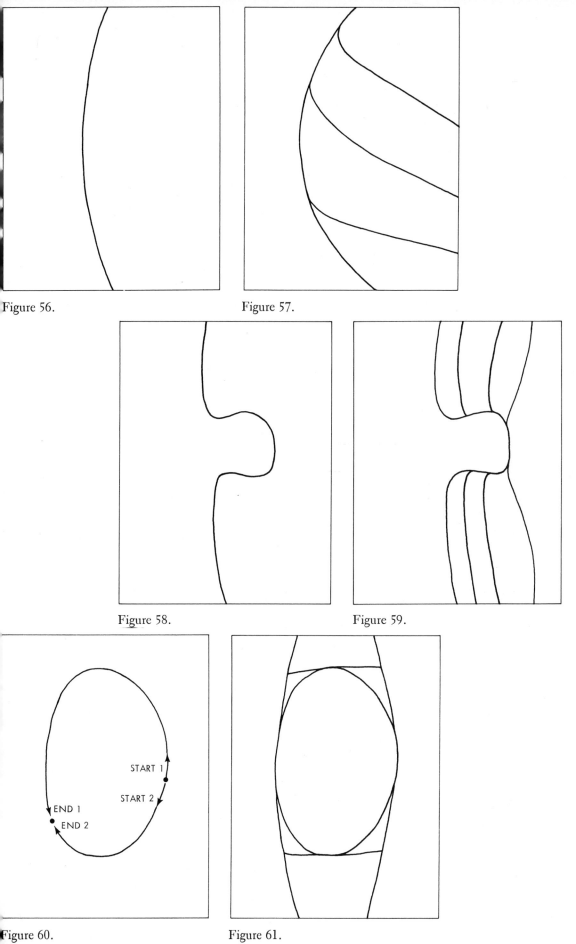

Figure 56.

Figure 57.

Figure 58.

Figure 59.

START 1

START 2

END 1

END 2

Figure 60.

Figure 61.

depends on the thickness of the glass and on the composition, takes about two and one half hours to come to the sagging temperature, which would be about 830° C (1526° F). The preferred sagging temperature depends really on the viscosity at high temperature and this depends on the composition. The correct sagging temperature can be determined experimentally, as we described earlier under "Testing the Glass."

The most important criterion is uniform temperature over the whole piece during the sagging step, so the piece deforms as planned, and also during the cooling step, for proper annealing. Thus the number and sizes of pieces fired at one time are determined by properties of the kiln and the desire to maintain uniform temperature over each piece. This may limit the heating rate, for too rapid heating produces temperature variations in the kiln.

After the glass has been sagged, the kiln is shut off. It can be cooled rapidly in the high temperature range, but then slowly in the annealing range, simply by having it closed properly. Massive pieces will require a controlled or programmed cooling. This is discussed in Appendix 2 under "Annealing."

DEVITRIFICATION OF GLASS

All glasses, if reheated and held at a certain temperature, which depends upon the composition, will crystallize. This process takes place more rapidly at the surface, and produces a haze. The ease with which this process takes place depends upon the composition. The most desirable glasses are those which do not crystallize rapidly when reheated. This subject is discussed in greater detail in Appendix 1.

It is important to select and test glasses for resistance to devitrification and surface hazing. Glasses which may be suitable for sagging and laminating may suffer too much crystallization for casting. Surface hazing can be minimized during sagging by coating with a transparent enamel, if no other glass can be substituted. There are glasses available for each of the forming techniques which will show virtually no hazing. Tests on commercially available glasses are described in the appendix.

FINISHING: USE OF EPOXIES

Some of the problems of sealing different colors together, when the different colors are also of different composition, have been mentioned under "Testing the Glass." This subject is discussed further in Appendix 1. The problems are fairly difficult and solutions sufficiently restrictive that other sealing techniques may open up new design possibilities. The use of epoxies represents a development that simply revolutionizes the working of glass. The three areas below represent design possibilities:

"Stained" glass windows

Window sections, laminated by fusing, can be sealed onto a transparent backing plate with epoxies and without the conventional leads. Sharp edges can be rounded first by firing.

Sagged-glass assemblages

Sections of sheet glass, or bottles, can be sagged in molds, and then assembled. It would be almost impossible to design molds to do this by fusing alone.

Laminated glass

Many layers of pieces of colored glass can be built up in a pattern-filling space, using epoxies, to a thickness impossible to achieve by fusing alone.

EXAMPLES: WORK OF ROBERT W. BROWN

Designs which do not use glass enamels or stains will of course be very simple. Such designs could be fused, but epoxies also can be used, especially if large areas of glass are involved. The first two of the designs by Robert Brown, of Glendale, California, make use of "hard edge" designs and very careful cutting to a design cartoon, with some smoothing of the edge with grinding stones (see Color Plates 5 through 8).

The next designs, also by Mr. Brown, show how parts of the assembled figures can be fired and sagged (or draped over the mold) and then mounted with epoxies (see Color Plates 9 and 10).

6. USING GLASS COLORS AND GLASS ENAMELS

INTRODUCTION

In an arbitrary way we have segregated the use of glass enamels and glass colors in this section. It is arbitrary because most of the glassworkers today combine the use of such colors with sagging or laminating. However, there is work being done today, mostly commercial in nature, in which the enamels or glass colors are purely decorative, and the glass is not deformed or changed in shape. The five classes of glass colors (see below) have a wide range of firing or maturing temperatures. The conditions of their application range from no deformation to the occurrence of sagging or bending. An example of enamel application without deformation was given in Figure 48. and, of course, all the Islamic mosque lamps and the goblets shown must have had enamel compositions such that there was no deformation.

GLASS COLORS AND GLASS ENAMELS

Glass decorating colors are basically low-melting borosilicate glasses colored with inorganic oxides. The subject of glass composition and colors is expanded upon in Sections 10 and 21. Enamels have the same basic composition as glass colors, but have an opacifying agent like titanium dioxide or molybdenum oxide. To the commercial decorators the term "glass color" is now a generic phrase and means any fusible coating for glass, including both the transparent colors and the opal colors. These colors are applied as fine powders and must be fused by heating the substrate and powder to the "maturing" point, which depends on temperature and time, just as in a glaze firing.

The glass colors may be divided into five classes ranging from low fire, called "soft," to high fire, sometimes called "hard." These terms are discussed further in Appendix 1 in the section "Use of 'Soft' and 'Hard' (Borosilicate) Glasses." The classes are:

1. Very Soft Colors: Not chemically resistant, high in lead oxide, low in opacity, limited color range, fired at 480–540°C (900–1000°F).
2. Soft Colors: Nonresistant, typical of line of colors for table glassware, fired at 540–580° C (1000–1080° F).
3. Soft Colors: Acid and sulfide resistant, fired at 590–600° C (1100–1120° F).
4. Resistant Colors: Alkali-resistant colors, used on commercial returnable bottles which are repeatedly washed in hot alkaline solutions, fired at 590–615° C (1100–1140° F).
5. High Fire Colors: Used on flat glass or bent glass, fired at 650–700° C (1200–1300° F) and accompanied by bending.

These glass-color classes are commercially available. One may of course mix glass colors using frits, much like formulating glazes.

There are three principal suspending mediums or vehicles for the glass colors. They are: water; water and denatured alcohol with some glycerin added; and turpentine. If water is used the glass must be very clean and free of oil and grease to avoid "crawling" of the applied glass colors. The water-and-alcohol mixture is used for white enamels so that decomposing oils will not discolor them during firing. A ratio of three or four parts of water to one of alcohol is adequate, and smooth application results if eleven ounces of glycerin is added to each gallon of the water-alcohol mixture. Turpentine is the most generally used vehicle. It evaporates rapidly and can be applied without crawling, to ware that is slightly oily or dirty from handling. For smooth application eight to twelve ounces of oil of copaiba is added to a gallon of turpentine.

In order to make the colors adhere better to the glass while in the air-dried state a hardening agent or binder is added. The addition of twelve to fifteen ounces of balsam of copaiba or dammar varnish to a gallon of turpentine will cause the colors to set hard when dry; if water-and-alcohol is the suspension medium, then sugar, gum tragacanth or gum arabic can be used as a binder. The exact amount can be determined only by experiment, because different colors have different physical properties. A minimum amount should be used because these organic materials must be burned out and can cause reduction. Generally, gum to the extent of .1 percent of the weight of the color is adequate.

Several of the companies which supply colors also supply the suspending vehicles, called "oils," in a variety of types. They range from water-insoluble to water-soluble, and also include thermofluids, which become fluid when heated and immediately solidify or freeze in contact with the glass. Technical bulletins can be obtained from such manufacturers.

SELECTION OF THE GLASS AND THE GLASS COLORS

We have already mentioned that there are some technical difficulties in sealing together different glasses—that is, glasses of different composition. This was mentioned in Section 4, "Physical Properties of Glass," and in Section 5, "Forming by Sagging and Laminating" in the part on "Selection of the Glass." In both sections we implied that the softening points (defined and discussed in Appendix 1) of the glasses to be sealed were approximately the same. Now, with the different classes of enamels and glass colors mentioned and defined, it is clear that there is a wide range of maturing temperatures—and therefore softening points. The selection of glass color depends on a design concept—that is, whether the artist wants his base glass, or substrate, to deform or not.

We see that several things must now match—the design concept must match the available glass forms (sheet glass, tubing, bottles), and the expansion coefficients and softening points of different colored glasses and of the enamels and glass colors must also match so that the design concept can be carried out and the final object kept free of stress.

Let us illustrate by forming a table of types of glass colors, glasses, expansion coefficients, and softening points (see Table 2). We may look at this table in a very elementary manner, avoiding for the moment technical definitions. We may observe that some enamels have lower softening points than some glasses; we may observe that some glasses are supposed to have matching coefficients and softening points within a group (made by a single manufacturer) but do not match another group. Further, two window glasses made by different companies (PPG Industries, Inc., and L-O-F), although made with great reproducibility, have different compositions and different physical properties. The range of softening points given by the Blenko Glass Company, Inc. as 700°–760°C indicates that for their enormous numbers of colored glasses there are variations.

TABLE 2:   SELECTION OF GLASS AND GLASS COLORS

Kind of Glass or Glass Color	Expansion Coefficient	Annealing Point (°C)	Softening Point (°C)
1. Glass Color—Class "1"*			480–540
2. Glass Color—Class "2"			540–580
3. Glass Color—Class "3"			590–600
4. Glass Color—Class "4"			590–615
5. Glass Color—Class "5"			650–700
6. PPG Industries, Inc., Pennvernon Sheet Glass	83×10^{-7}/°C	553	733
7. L-O-F, Colburn Sheet Glass	88.2×10^{-7}/°C	514	727
8. Blenko Glass Company, Colored Sheet Glass	95×10^{-7}/°C (Calculated)	538	760
9. Kokomo Opalescent Glass Company, Colored Sheet Glass	92×10^{-7}/°C	511	677
10. Paul Wissmach Company, Inc., Colored Sheet Glass	Data not measured by company		
11. Leo Popper, Inc., Colored Sheet Glass	No data available on European colored glass		
12. CGW, 8391, Clear Optical Glass	89×10^{-7}/°C	440	601

* For the glass colors, the softening point listed is really a "maturing range."

We can begin to use the table in the following manner. It will be straightforward to use commercial glass colors on a window-glass composition, either that of PPG Industries, Inc. (Pennvernon process sheet glass), or L-O-F (Colburn process sheet glass), provided one obtains the proper commercial glass colors. These two glasses, of expansion coefficient in the range O–300°C, given as 83 x 10^{-7}cm/cm/°C. and 88.2 x 10^{-7}cm/cm/°C should have slightly different formulations of glass colors.

The commercial colored glasses (Blenko, Kokomo, and Paul Wissmach) have different glass properties than do the window glasses. The properties are available for Blenko and Kokomo glasses. They will need different glass colors than do the window glasses. The glass colors must be of higher expansion and are adjusted by the color manufacturer or the craftsman by mixing the color frit with a flux (which can be purchased from the color manufacturer). The flux will increase the expansion. Most of the color manufacturers indicate they have formulations to match these glasses.

On closer examination of the physical properties of these glasses (see Appendix 1, "Some Physical Properties of Glass"), it is apparent that the compositions of a given manufacturer have not been adjusted to give identical properties. The softening points of different colors are different, and that is indicative of other differences, like expansion. The properties listed in the table represent an average property which may vary among the different colors.

Testing Different Glasses and Glass Colors

Our recommendation is to use standard glasses with known properties and standard enamels and glass colors with known properties, and to choose systems with matching properties. The testing procedures recommended before in Section 5 under "Testing the Glass" can be used, but additional use of enamels or glass colors complicates or compounds the problem.

Therefore it is necessary to turn to the manufacturers of the glasses and get physical properties from them (expansion coefficient, softening point, annealing point) and then turn to the enamel and glass-color manufacturer for the preferred compositions or recommendations for adjusting the compositions by the addition of flux.

One can work with small test specimens, checking to see if the enamels "spall" off or crack. This would reveal large mismatch of properties. One can check the relative expansion of the different glasses used, considering one as a standard (the window glasses would make good standards), and by various cross-checks build up a table of expansions for different colors. The relative-expansion test is described in Appendix 1.

Application of Glass Colors

Glass colors may be applied by painting, spraying, dusting, stamping, or printing with silk screens. For painting, the colors are worked into a pasty

53

consistency, using the turpentine mixture. For spraying, a thin creamy consistency is desired, with 4 to 4½ ounces of turpentine per pound of color.

Before the glass is decorated it should be sanded on the edges with wet emery paper. It is desirable to sand right after cutting, for the edges are extremely sharp. Cotton work gloves are useful to minimize cutting the fingers. The sanding enables one to better handle the glass, and also produces a better-rounded edge after the firing. After sanding, the glass should be washed with a good detergent or cleaner and dried carefully, keeping the surface to be decorated clean.

Then the glass is decorated by painting or spraying or some other technique. Decoration is closely linked with design and is a subject which would fill a book. The examples below show a few of many possibilities, but serve as suggestions for the use of glass colors to enhance sagged and laminated glass.

After decorating, the glass is lifted by the fingertips and placed, properly centered, in the mold. The mold is placed in the kiln for firing. Cleanliness is very important and the inside of the kiln should be brushed or vacuum-cleaned first. When the kiln is used for both ceramics and glass, two sets of shelves, one for the glass and the other for the ceramics, are desirable.

The more modern printing screens are no longer silk, but stainless steel, nylon or Orlon. The stainless steel is necessary for the "hot oil" or thermo-fluid medium; the nylon and Orlon give longer life than the silk.

Heating Cycles

Just as for sagging and laminating, the heating cycle for enameling is straightforward, like a bisque firing. Either an electric or a gas-fired kiln may be used. There are three steps; heating to the maturing temperature of the enamels or glass colors, or to the saging temperature, whichever controls the process; cooling to the annealing temperature; then slow cooling to room temperature. The annealing process and the overall heating cycles are discussed in greater detail in Appendix 2.

Finishing

Just as was explained in the previous discussion on finishing in Section 5, several things can be done with pieces, using a combination of techniques involving sagging or laminating with enamels and glass colors. The final result can be much like a painting, closely resembling a collage or serigraph.

Examples: Work of Robert W. Brown

Several examples by Robert W. Brown, of Glendale, California, show this painting quality. These examples are windows and panels in the Valley Jewish Community Center and Temple in North Hollywood. The work is shown in Color Plates 11 through 19. Other examples of his work, a door panel and a crest, are shown in Color Plates 20 through 22.

7. FORMING BY MOLD-FUSING

INTRODUCTION

The technique of mold-fusion lies between laminating and casting. It is possible to look at it as simply a derivative of laminating, but from a historical point of view, as was mentioned in Section 3, it existed in ancient times. Laminating, which depends on the use of flat glass or fragments of flat glass, is a modern development. The presentation here will stress this historical aspect and will review the studies, made earlier for The Corning Museum of Glass, on ancient techniques. Thus the different steps discussed below—mold materials, shaping the molds, etc.—will be presented briefly and then expanded in greater detail in the next section, on mold-casting. It is this latter technique that offers so much more to the craftsman in terms of design potential than mold-fusing or even conventional laminating (unless the freedom of epoxies is explored), so that major emphasis will be placed on mold-casting.

MOLD MATERIALS AND MOLDS

(See Section 8 under "Mold Materials" and "Forming the Molds")

SHAPING THE MOLDS—DESIGN RESTRICTIONS

The molds to be used in fusing glass are shaped by conventional plaster-working methods, or a model in clay or wax can be invested. The real problem is the design restrictions, which depend on the form of the glass to be placed in the mold. Mold-fusion, wherein the glass is prearranged in a pattern and will fuse with little flow, stands in contrast to casting, wherein the glass flows appreciably. Thus in a shallow open mold, the arranged bits of glass will fuse and sag downward without destroying the pattern. If the mold is a deep hollow, like a bowl, the glass must be restrained from "folding over." This will be made clearer below, with specific examples.

TESTING THE GLASS

Two of the physical properties should match for mold-fusing: first, the coefficient of thermal expansion must match to minimize stress; second, the softening point should match so that the pattern deforms in a consistent manner. These properties are described in greater detail in Appendix 1, with a discussion of testing the glass, and preliminary remarks on testing have been presented in Sections 5 and 6.

ARRANGING GLASS CANES OR MARBLES

An illustration of the design problems will prove most useful. In an attempt to replicate an ancient Roman-Alexandrian fused mosaic bowl, small sections of patterned canes were placed in a hemispherical plaster-sand mold. This mold had been cast over a clay model; then mold and clay were separated and the mold was washed clean. The appearance of the small sections of glass, which were then placed in the mold, is shown in Figure 62. The first attempt to heat this glass for fusing was done in the open bowl. After fusing, one side folded over and sagged down, as might have been predicted.

A two-piece mold was then made, using a clay model and a "separator" at the upper edge. The clay model had the desired wall thickness of the final fused bowl. The small sections of patterned canes had irregular lengths; after placing them in the bowl the inner mold rested on the canes slightly raised above the rim of the outer mold. As the glass deformed while fusing, the inner mold dropped into place. This is illustrated in Figures 63 and 64, which show the initial arrangement, the final form in the mold, and the bowl removed from the mold.

One may think of mold-fusion patterns as of three general types: arranged in layers parallel to the mold surface, as in laminating; arranged in elements perpendicular to the surface, as with small sections of canes; and arranged in space, like stacking marbles, so that there is a three-dimensional pattern. Spherical marbles stacked fuse together to make a polyhedron with many flat surfaces.

HEATING THE MOLDS

The molds (with glass inside) are heated slowly to drive off the water, held for a while at 100°C, then heated slowly to 300°C to drive off the chemically bound water, and finally heated to the fusing temperature. This temperature depends upon the physical properties of the glass, and would be close to the softening point or somewhat above to speed up the process. After fusion the temperature is lowered to the annealing point, held there awhile, and then molds and glass are cooled slowly to room temperature. The cycles for heating and cooling, and the principles involved, will be described in greater detail in Section 8 and in the appendix.

FINISHING THE OBJECT

In general, there will be part of the object that has a free edge, not in contact with a mold, that may be irregular. Unless such irregularity is part of your design, it will require grinding, using a grinding mill and abrasive. This is discussed further in Section 11, "Grinding Equipment."

EXAMPLES: DUPLICATION OF ANCIENT BOWLS

The steps required to make a shallow bowl may be listed as follows:

1. Make the model: The core can be made by "wet forming" of plaster-sand directly, using a primitive lathe and template, or by form-

Figure 62.
Arranging
mosaic canes for
mold-fusing.

Figure 63. Cane arrangement and fused bowl.

Figure 64. Mold
with inner mold
in place and
fused bowl
removed.

ing the inside of the bowl in clay and casting the plaster-sand mixture in it. The top edge must be designed so as to rest later on the lip of the outside.

2. With core complete, the model is built up on the core in wax, or clay, using a thin sheet of either one.
3. The outside mold is cast against this, with a separator between regions where mold contacts mold.
4. The wax is then melted out and the molds are separated, or the molds are separated and the clay is removed.
5. Short canes of glass, of length equal to the wall thickness of the model or only slightly longer, are arranged in the mold.
6. Put core in place.
7. Heat molds and glass in furnace to fusing temperature; the glass deforms slightly and the inner core drops down into place so that both sides of the bowl are in contact with the mold.
8. Cool.
9. Remove and grind and polish edges.

Example: Venini Shallow Bowl

The details of making this bowl are not known, but we may describe how it could be made using mold-fusing techniques:

1. Make a model for casting the inside. Cast the mold mixture and then remove clay.
2. Build up the model on the inner core, using a rolled sheet of clay of the proper thickness.
3. Cast outside using separator in regions where molds contact each other.
4. Separate and remove clay.
5. Put short canes of glass in place.
6. Put inner core in place (the function of the inner core in a shallow design is to deform both surfaces and avoid irregularities).
7. Heat molds and glass to fusing temperature.
8. Cool.
9. Remove and grind and polish edges if necessary.

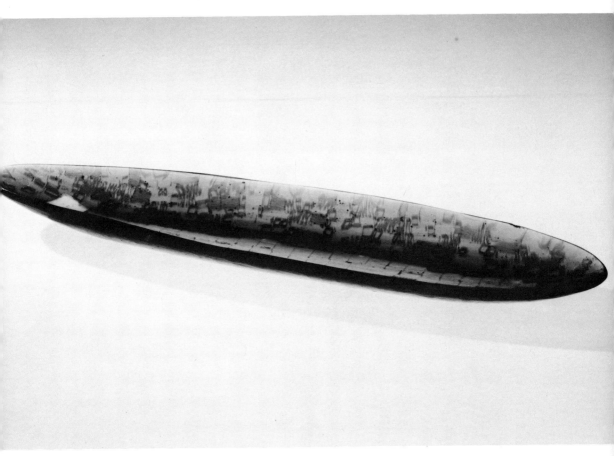

Figure 65. Shallow tray designed by Venini. (Corning Museum of Glass)

8. FORMING BY MOLD-CASTING

INTRODUCTION

The technique of mold-casting is to be considered the most advanced of the glassforming techniques discussed in this book. Mold-casting of glass. like metal casting, has practically no limitations on design, at least with properly designed molds and vents. As was discussed in the historical section in Part One, mold-casting preceded free-blowing and was used for a variety of shapes from shallow bowls to reliefs to sculptures. With limited technical knowledge, the Egyptian craftsman, for example, used procedures which were basically simple, even though they might have been very time-consuming. While the process is simple, actual practice involves designing models and making molds with an understanding of the overall process, so the design concept can be executed in the most effective manner. Many craftsmen will have had analogous practice in making molds for ceramics or for casting metal for jewelry or sculpture. For those who have had no previous experience, the following discussion on molds will explain the processes and steps.

MOLD MATERIALS

A mold material, which can be a mixture, should have the following properties: It should have a plastic period, or be castable; it should then become rigid and fairly strong; it should be refractory; it should not crack upon firing; it should not change dimensions or shrink very much; and, finally, it should be fairly weak, even water-soluble, after firing.

The formula developed by Frederick Carder was:

> 1 part plaster of Paris
> 1 part very fine silica (200 mesh)
> 1 part crushed "burnt" mixture of above two.

This mixture is plastic, castable, fairly strong when prepared with conventional plaster-mixing techniques, and quite weak and friable after being heated to 900–1000°C. We replaced the burnt mixture with fine silica so that the proportion of plaster to silica was 1:2. Molds of these mixtures must be heated slowly from room temperature to 100°C, held there for several hours, then slowly heated to 300°C. There were some problems with cracking, so we investigated other mixtures, all of which are more expensive than this mixture. These experiments are described later in this section under "Investigation of Mold Materials and Commercial Glasses," and the results are summarized below.

We studied, first, special plaster products of the United States Gypsum Company, namely Hydrocal and Ultracal. Following that, we studied Hydroperm, which is used for metal casting. The key to the cracking problem is firing shrinkage, and these materials used alone show much shrinkage—most with Ultracal, less with Hydrocal, and least with Hydroperm, which already has some refractory added to it. We balanced the Ultracal and developed mixtures much like Frederick Carder's, namely:

and
$$
\begin{array}{l}
\text{1 part Hydrocal} \\
\text{2 parts fine silica} \\
\\
\text{3 parts Hydroperm} \\
\text{1 part very fine silica}
\end{array}
$$

The latter mixture could be changed to 1:1 to decrease the cost, as the Hydroperm is more expensive than the silica.

Both of these mixtures, made with conventional plaster-forming techniques, but without great care to develop maximum density and maximum "green" strength (by weighing carefully), do produce stronger green and fired molds than the casting plaster-silica mixture. We use these because we have fewer problems with them than with the casting plaster-silica.

Modeling the Form in Clay or Wax

A model must be made in some material which is convenient to form and which lends itself to the mold-making step. The two most suitable materials are clay and wax. We prefer clay, not on any rational, well-thought-out basis, but more because we like the "feel" of clay, particularly one with a little grog in it. The amounts of clay used are small and inexpensive, so that one can be careless or make major changes or start over.

The clay is purchased from a ceramic supply house ready to use, packed in a 25-pound size in a plastic bag. It is usually in a soft plastic condition, suitable for roughing out a shape quickly, but usually too plastic to support a tall shape, and somewhat sticky, so that it is difficult to finish smoothly. So the shape is roughed out and permitted to dry a little.

Then when the clay is in a medium plastic condition, the object can be finished, even with the application of more clay, and the surface can be smoothed nicely. Do not let it dry to a stiff plastic condition, as then it will be difficult to get the clay out of the mold.

One can form the clay in any convenient manner. It is critical to eliminate trapped air from a clay shape that has to be fired. However, for model making one may have the clay hollow, or with interior bubbles or holes, as it is only the surface in contact with the investment material which is important. One can cut the clay, carve it with knives and other clay-working tools, shape it by squeezing, rolling, pressing together with other pieces, using slabs, draping sheets over molds, pinching, and, in fact, any convenient method. Such methods are discussed in books on clay sculpture or on pottery. A book

61

on sculpture by Frank Eliscu (*Sculpture in Clay, Wax and Slate*, Chilton Book Company, Philadelphia, 1959) is to be recommended for both clay and wax, while one on pottery by F. H. Norton (*Ceramics for the Artist Potter*, Addison-Wesley Publishing Company, Inc., Cambridge, 1956) is to be recommended for clay.

The conventional procedure in model making and mold making is to complete the model first, then go through the steps of making the molds, which might be in two, three or more pieces. It may be simpler to combine the two processes stepwise: Make part of the model up to a good "dividing" line and cast the first piece mold; continue with the next part, and cast the second piece mold against the first and the model; make the next part of the model and cast the third piece mold against the second and the model. This would require strong powers of visualization, because part of the model will be hidden during this process.

The alternate method is to work in wax. This method is more difficult in the modeling stage and simpler in the mold-making stage. Various waxes are available today under names like "precision pattern wax," "plastic," "casting," "carving," "industrial," etc. They have very uniform properties and are available in different grades of hardness or the temperature at which they can be worked. They also have a low thermal expansion coefficient. This is important because the wax is going to be melted out of the investment material in the waste-wax process and, in heating, a wax with a high expansion coefficient would break the mold before the wax became fluid. The wax is purchased from an investment casting supply house and comes in a variety of extruded shapes—round, half round, square, rectangular, etc., or in sheets.

Wax permits a wide range of shapes and can be bent, twisted, formed, and reformed, much like clay. Beeswax was used in ancient times, either to form an object (some of which have been discovered in Egyptian tombs), or to make a model for the waste-wax process. The Greeks, the Romans, and the Italian masters of the Renaissance all worked in wax. Theophilus describes working in wax: "If you want to fix handles on the chalice, as soon as you have beaten and scraped it, and before doing any other work on it, take some wax and from it form the handles, and sculpt on them dragons or animals, or birds, or foliage in whatever way you like." (Book III, Chapter XXX, "Casting Handles for the Chalice.") He then goes on to describe investing the wax in clay, melting out the wax, and casting the silver. Giorgio Vasari, in 1550, published an introduction to his *Lives of the Most Eminent Painters, Sculptors, and Architects* which describes the sculptor's use of wax to make a small preliminary model and the bronze caster's use of wax to create a thin-walled shell for casting large bronze figures. (Vasari: *On Technique*, Dover Publications, Inc., 1960, N.Y.)

To make a wax model, the wax is shaped with the fingers and with modeling tools. It must be softened somewhat, using a source of gentle heat (like the palm of the hand). Two pieces are joined by pressure or by touching the blade of a knife, preheated in a flame, to both surfaces where they touch. When the little line of melted wax hardens again, the two pieces will be joined.

Forming the Molds

The materials, plaster and sand, are purchased in 100-pound sacks. The plaster must be stored in a dry place, and the sack closed carefully after usage, to keep it dry. The materials can be premixed, dry, according to the proportion desired and then added to the water, just as in working with plaster alone, or the plaster can be added to the water first and then to the sand, in the proper proportions.

There are excellent discussions in brochures from the United States Gypsum Company, and in books on ceramics like F. H. Norton's *Ceramics for the Artist Potter*, Addison-Wesley Publishing Company, Inc., Cambridge, Massachusetts (1956), or in books on industrial model making like R. R. Knoblaugh's *Model Making for Industrial Design*, McGraw-Hill, New York (1958). Briefly, a fairly deep plastic container, slightly flexible to aid in cleaning, should be used to hold water in the required amount. The materials are sifted a handful at a time onto the surface of the water, where they wet and sink. Avoid dumping the materials into the water. This addition is continued until all of the free water at the surface is taken up by the mixture. As there is no great effort made to produce molds of highest density and greatest strength, these methods of determining the ratio of plaster-sand mixture to water are adequate. For making molds requiring strength and density, proper proportions of plaster and water are attained by weighing. Such proportions are given in the brochures for each type of plaster: casting, Hydrocal, etc.

After letting the mixture stand for two minutes, stir it with the hand beneath the surface, with a rolling motion. Make sure there are no stagnant regions by reaching down into the lower part of the container and even sweeping the hand across the bottom. Stir for two minutes.

Then one is ready to pour the plaster-sand mixture into another container for investing the model. The model can be resting on a flat board covered with a thin sheet of plastic. The model is enclosed in a dam made of clay, or a coiled sheet of linoleum with the lower outside edge sealed with clay. The mixture is poured over the model and fills the space between model and dam, eventually covering the model and forming a flat surface which will be the base during firing. If one waits awhile for the plaster-sand mixture to reach the "plastic" state, then the mixture can be shaped by "wet-forming." Make sure that the mold has a thickness of about ½ inch in the thinnest region. Let the plaster stand until rigid enough to lift, meanwhile cleaning and washing the plastic mixing container. When the plaster-sand mixture is fairly rigid, strip off the dam material, give the edges a slight bevel to prevent them from being chipped later, pull out the clay model (if it is a simple relief) or prepare to remove it by cutting it out and washing with a jet of water. If the model is wax it will be melted out later. Clean up the linoleum and other work tools.

In general, the design of the mold or molds is similar to that for metal casting. Thus one can use a simple one-piece mold for investing a relief, or several-piece molds for a clay object, or the waste-wax investment method for a model made in wax, or, finally, one can shape and carve the mold material directly. If the completed molds do consist of several pieces, then the pieces are assembled, covered with more plaster to seal the joints (after thorough wetting), and wrapped with a steel wire to minimize separation if a crack should open up. The molds are designed to have a large opening and cuplike space at the top to hold the amount of glass required to complete the casting (unless you wish to add glass, when at the casting temperature, through a furnace porthole).

One-Piece Molds

One-piece molds are very straightforward. A typical example would be a mold of a relief. The relief should be built up to considerable thickness, like 1 inch, so that there will be space to hold the raw glass required to complete the casting. The relief is simply invested with the mold material, and after setting up, the clay is stripped out and the mold cleaned. Upon placing it in the furnace, with the cuplike space up, one can see that the relief is really cast upside down, and the rear surface will be smooth.

Piece Molds

Piece molds, consisting of two, three, or more pieces, are more complex. One must select a "parting" line and build up a surface along that line, extending out from the model. The mold material is cast over the model and against that extended surface. This surface can be made by sticking thin strips of flexible brass into the model along the parting line, trimming the outer edge with a shears, to make it regular and completing a vertical dam with linoleum and clay. Or the surface can be made with clay, shaped and modeled to go along the parting line.

After part of the mold is cast, the brass strips are removed, or the clay surface is removed, the model touched up, the mold edge cleaned up and a separating agent applied where the next piece mold will touch the first. The process is repeated for the next mold section with a new separating line established on the model. The second piece mold is cast against the model and between the first mold and the extended surface at the new separating line, built out from the model as before.

After the pieces are complete, they are removed from the model and cleaned. They are reassembled and invested with additional mold material, ready for casting glass.

Shaping Terra-Cotta Forms

Plaster models can be made either by casting over a clay form or by working directly during the plastic period. Here casting plaster or Hydrocal is used. The mold is cleaned and dried. Terra-cotta can be pressed against that mold, after being rolled out into a slab about ¾ of an inch thick. Upon drying slightly, the clay is removed, and the surface can be textured with various tools. These forms are used for sagging glass. After careful drying and bisque firing, the form is sprayed with a thin coating of a separator. Various separators can be used: whiting (calcium carbonate), talc, alumina hydrate, feldspar, mixtures of 200 mesh silica and EPK china clay, or commercial separators.

PREPARATION OF THE GLASS

Amount of Glass

For most work, glass ranging in size from coarse powders to marbles is desired. If only one color is being used, the pieces can be as large as chunks or fragments several inches across. Marbles and small bits of glass are available commercially; sheet glass or rod can be broken up using the mosaic tile cutters. Sheet glass can be scribed with the glass cutter and then broken, while rod can be scratched with the triangular file and broken. Glass can be crushed with a hammer on metal plates. It is advisable to wear safety glasses.

To estimate the amount of glass needed, one really has to know the volume of glass required to fill the mold. One may get this volume of glass directly by filling the mold with water, pouring it from a graduated cylinder. The mold has to be very damp before doing this. One may get the volume indirectly by knowing the mass or the weight of clay (or wax) used in making the original model, and converting this mass (or weight) into volume. This conversion involves knowing the mass density or weight density, a quantity that you determine:

$$\text{Mass density} = \rho = \frac{\text{mass (grams)}}{\text{volume (cm}^3)}$$

$$\text{Weight density} = D = \frac{\text{weight (pounds)}}{\text{volume (ft}^3)}$$

If one uses the metric system of units, then the mass is in grams; if one uses the British system of units, then the weight is in pounds.

After determining the density of the wet clay (which will depend on the degree of dryness), the volume can then be computed from the mass or the weight:

$$\text{Volume (cm}^3\text{)} = \text{Density}\big/\text{Mass (grams)}$$
$$V_{required} = \rho_{clay} \times m_{clay}$$

Now that the volume to be filled with glass is known, the density of the glass is determined experimentally, as above. Once that is determined, the mass of glass is calculated from the above volume and density of glass:

$$m_{glass} = \rho_{glass} \times V_{required}$$

For example, the volume of one mold was found to be 412 cm³ (actually 412 milliliters, but they are about the same). The density of the glass was 3.58 grams/cm³; the mass of glass is then 1475 grams.

Type of Glass

There are only three conditions as to type of glass. The glass should have a moderately low softening point, so that the casting temperature is on the low side. This would rule out the low-expansion borosilicate glass used for flame-working. Second, the glass should not crystallize or devitrify. The glass will have to be tested for that and abandoned if unsatisfactory. Devitrification is discussed in Appendix 1. Finally, if mixtures of different colors are used, their coefficients of thermal expansion and softening points must match, as described below under "Working with Colors" and in Appendix 1.

Cleaning the Glass

The glass must be free of dirt. This cleaning can usually be done by washing with detergent and water before the glass is broken up. Further, if there are areas which have been ground, they must be discarded when the glass is broken up, or they will cause a streaky pattern in the casting.

HEATING THE MOLD, ADDITION OF THE GLASS, AND COOLING THE MOLD

The mold is placed in the furnace and glass may be added immediately if the model was made in clay. If the model was made in wax, the mold is placed in the kiln upside down, the wax is melted out and runs to a cool region. Then the mold is cooled and turned over so glass can be added later.

In either case the mold is preheated slowly to 100°C to drive off water. The temperature is raised to 300°C to remove bound water and if wax has been used, it is raised to 600°C to burn out organic residue. Then glass can be added through a port in the furnace door as the temperature of the furnace increases to the casting temperature. The glass is placed in the space or well at the top of the mold, using a long-handled tongs or a small ladle with a

66

long handle. As the glass softens and flows down, more is added until the measured amount has been reached, or until one can determine visually that enough has been added. The furnace is then cooled through the annealing cycle.

FINISHING THE OBJECT

After mold and object are cooled, they are removed from the furnace, the mold is broken away from the object, and the glass is washed and dried. Various imperfections like moldmarks or "sprues" are removed by sawing with the cutoff saw and then by grinding. Bench grinders with rubber-abrasive wheels can be used dry; other types—laps and wheels—are used wet. Following this, other finishing methods are polishing and acid-polishing.

WORKING WITH COLORS

One of the most exciting aspects of the casting technique is the use of color and the effects which are obtained in this unique manner. When small bits of glasses of different colors are placed in the well above the mold, they fuse together and flow down forming flow patterns of great complexity.

These glasses must match with respect to the thermal coefficient of expansion and also the softening point. This is discussed in Appendix 1 in detail. We have not explored this area in any depth, but it is clear that systematic studies could be made, much like glaze studies, with varying ratios of colors. However, the design of the molds and the well will have an effect on the patterns produced, so that the studies should involve sets of identical castings.

FIRST SCULPTURE: THE DECORATIVE RELIEF

Reliefs have great appeal, with stylized monograms (see Figure 4) or calligraphic designs having special appeal (see Section 16, "Casting Shapes"). A very simple design has been chosen to illustrate the steps in making a variety of reliefs. The steps are as follows:

1. Make a model in clay, built up on a slablike modeled base (see Figure 66).

Figure 66. Clay model of a relief.

2. Cast the mold material over it, using the linoleum dam, sealed with clay at the lower edge and at the overlapping seam (see Figures 67 through 69).

Figure 67. *Model surrounded by linoleum dam.*

Figure 68. *Investing model with mold material.*

Figure 69. *Model completely invested.*

3. Strip off linoleum when mold material is set up, turn over and strip out the clay, bevel edge of mold, and clean the mold with a jet of water (see Figures 70 and 71). Measure volume of water equal to glass required. Let air-dry (Figure 72).

Figure 70. *Stripping clay from mold.*

Figure 71. *Cleaning mold (beveling upper edge).*

Figure 72. *Air-dried mold.*

69

Figure 73. *Mold and glass in casting furnace.*

4. Place mold in furnace; place proper (by weight) amount of glass in mold (see Figure 73).

Figure 74. *Mold and cast glass in furnace.*

5. Heat to casting temperature—slowly at the beginning to complete drying of the mold and removal of the bound water. Then cool to annealing temperature and follow annealing schedule (see Appendix 2).
6. Cool to room temperature (see Figure 74) and remove from the furnace; break mold away from the glass (see Figure 75).

Figure 75. *Breaking mold material away from glass.*

70

7. Clean up the glass by washing, and grind base where needed. The finished object is shown in Figure 76.

Figure 76. *Finished relief.*

Examples of reliefs, all done with the same technique, are shown in Figures 77 through 80 and in color plates 24 and 25.

Figure 77. *"Sun-Burst."*

Figure 78. *"Fish."*

Figure 80. *"Flower."*

Figure 79. *"Wheel of Life."*

Second Sculpture: The Shallow Bowl with Decorative Relief

Shallow bowls have been of interest to us in the past, from the time of the studies on the ancient bowls made by casting methods. They represent a more difficult operation than casting the relief—slightly more difficult if the bowl is shallow and having increasing difficulty in freeing the clay with increasing depth of the model. It simply requires more patience and time. The steps are as follows:

1. Make a model and mount it on a large tapered base which will later be the container for the raw chunk glass (see Figure 81).

Figure 81. *Model of shallow bowl.*

2. Cast the mold over the model, using the linoleum dam, sealed with clay at the lower edges and on the overlapping seam (see Figures 82 and 83).

Figure 82. *Model surrounded by linoleum dam.*

Figure 83. *Initial stages of investing the model.*

3. Strip off linoleum when mold material has set up, bevel the edges of the mold, remove clay and wash out mold (see Figures 84 and 85). Let air-dry (see Figure 86).

Figure 84. *Removing clay from mold.*

Figure 85. *Beveling edges of mold.*

73

4. Place mold in furnace with measured amount of glass in the "well," and heat slowly to dry the mold and remove bound water. Heat to casting temperature.
5. Cool to annealing temperature and follow annealing program.

Figure 86. *Dried mold.*

6. Cool to room temperature, remove, and break mold away. Clean mold out of the interior. Wash off glass and grind any sharp parts (see Figure 87).

The finished object is shown in Figure 88.

Figure 87. *Breaking mold away from glass.*

Figure 88. *Finished bowl with relief.*

Third Sculpture: Cubic Crystal

A whole series of shapes which resemble natural crystals, but have curved surfaces and projections or indentations, have interesting design possibilities in glass. The steps to make a crystal three inches on a side are given below. If the crystal were any larger, it would be made hollow to keep the wall thickness one inch or less and to simplify annealing. The hollow crystal would require several extra steps.

74

1. Make a model of the crystal and place it on a tapered base which will serve as a well to hold the chunk glass (see Figure 89).

Figure 89. *Model of cubic crystal.*

2. Enclose in the linoleum dam (see Figure 90) and invest with the mold material (see Figures 91 and 92).

Figure 90. *Model enclosed in linoleum dam.*

Figure 91. *Investing the model.*

75

Figure 92. *Model completely invested with mold material.*

Figure 93. *Removing the clay.*

3. Strip off the linoleum when the mold material is set up, and pull out the clay at the top (Figure 93). Shape the top well with a knife (Figure 94).

Figure 94. *Shaping the well at the top.*

76

Figure 95. *The cleaned mold.*

4. Clean out all of the clay (Figure 95), measure the volume of glass required, weigh and add the glass to the well, and place in the furnace (see Figure 96).

Figure 96. *Mold and glass in furnace.*

5. Cast the glass, anneal, let cool to room temperature and break away the mold (see Figure 97).
The finished object is shown in Figure 98.

Figure 97. *Breaking the mold material away from the glass.*

Figure 98. *Cubic crystal.*

Investigation of Mold Materials and Commercial Glasses

The mold mixture for glass fusing and glass casting developed by Frederick Carder was:

100 casting plaster + 100 fine silica (200 mesh)

or:

100 plaster + 100 fine silica + 100 burned crushed mixture

The latter was preferred.

It was not clear why he had developed these particular mixtures nor why he had studied other additives to the plaster (clays, for example). We started to review the mixtures, especially because the first mixture frequently cracked.

We thought that the casting plaster could be replaced by other special plasters, like Hydrocal or Ultracal, products of the United States Gypsum Company. We thought, further, that we could better understand cracking by studying mixtures like those shown in Table 3. We used casting plaster, Hydrocal, or Ultracal in formulas ranging from no silica to 33 percent plaster

TABLE 3:   STUDIES ON MOLD MATERIALS

Constitu-	Mixtures					
ents	I	II	III	IV	V	VI
Plaster*	100	80	60	50	40	33
Silica	0	20	40	50	60	67

* Either Casting Plaster, Hydrocal, or Ultracal

and 67 percent silica. Such mixtures would exaggerate effects. We prepared disks seven inches in diameter and about two inches thick.

We heated slowly to 100°C, held for several hours, then increased slowly to 300°C during the drying process. Then the temperature was increased to 1000°C. We observed that the 100 Hydrocal, 100 Ultracal, and 100 casting plaster all showed such extreme shrinkage when fired to 1000°C that each broke up into small pieces. The Ultracal showed most shrinkage and we did not study that anymore. As the proportion of silica increased, the shrinkage decreased, and the cracks were fewer and finer. Mixtures of 50-50 were critical; sometimes they cracked, sometimes not. Most of the shrinkage occurred above 600°C (particularly above 800°C).

We obtained brochures from the United States Gypsum Company on their different plasters, and discovered Hydroperm, a plaster-refractory mixture used for metal casting. It is more porous than casting plaster (it has a high permeability) and therefore can be dried more easily, a prerequisite for casting metal. We reasoned that the higher porosity would also produce low shrinkage. Experiments showed the following results (the measurements are crude and all column IV's are essentially the same):

TABLE 4:   FIRING SHRINKAGE OF PLASTER-SILICA MIXTURES

Kind of Plaster	Shrinkage (Percent)			
	I*	II	III	IV
Casting	7.0	2.0	0.85	0.8
Hydrocal	6.5	3.0	1.7	0.8
Hydroperm	2.8	1.7	1.7	0.9

* I 100:0, II 67:33 III 50:50 IV 33:67

The fired Hydroperm-silica mixtures were stronger than the corresponding ones with Hydrocal or casting plaster, and the 100 Hydroperm showed little cracking, while the others definitely needed the addition of silica.

We conclude that suitable mixtures are:

> 50 Hydroperm + 50 silica ranging to 75 Hydroperm + 25 silica
> 33 Hydrocal + 67 silica
> 33 casting plaster + 67 silica

We like to work with the 75 Hydroperm, 25 silica, but of course the casting plaster is much less expensive.

We also made studies comparing the properties of commercially available glasses. These studies covered:

> Softening points by sagging bars
> Relative softening points of different glasses
> Sealing of sheet glasses
> Surface tension rounding of edges
> Casting temperatures
> Relative casting temperatures of different glasses (by casting four
>   different glasses, in four different molds, with the same firing cycle)
> Devitrification

We really wanted to establish the viscosities at which these processes took place (see Appendix 1, "Viscosity Coefficient and Temperature"). The glasses studied were:

> Corning Glass Works Code 8430 chunk
> PPG Industries Pennvernon process sheet window glass
> L-O-F Colburn process sheet window glass
> Blenko Glass Company sheet and chunk, clear and colored
> Kokomo Opalescent Glass Company sheet, clear and colored
> Paul Wissmach Glass Company cullet, colored

The results are described in various sections related to the studies, mostly in Appendix 1. General observations are:

1. Glasses with trapped bubbles (like "antique" glasses) may produce large bubbles during casting (Blenko, Kokomo).
2. The window glasses show considerable surface devitrification during casting, making them quite unsuitable.
3. The colored glasses from a given company do not really match in physical properties.
4. Colored glasses show more surface devitrification than the Corning Glass Works Code 8430, but the Blenko and Kokomo glasses are quite satisfactory. The Paul Wissmach glasses show excessive crystallization.

We recommend working with Blenko glasses and Kokomo glasses, but point out that tests should be conducted even on these.

ꝑart Three|Forming Equipment

9. FURNACES

There are two classes of furnaces available: gas-fired and electric. As the upper temperature required for work with soft glass is 1000°C, which is not particularly demanding, there are many different types or models of ceramic kilns available which can be adapted. The choice depends on three factors:

1. Annealing requirements
2. Number and size of pieces with each firing
3. Technique of adding the glass—before firing or during firing.

The annealing requirements, which will be discussed in detail in Appendix 2, can be understood in terms of a generalized heating cycle curve, which includes an initial portion for sagging, laminating, fusing, or casting, followed by annealing. The temperature is plotted against time (see Figure 99):

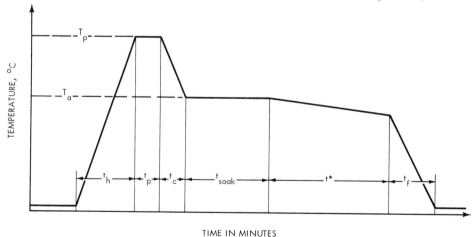

TIME IN MINUTES

Figure 99. Generalized heating cycle.

81

After the initial step, all of the glass should be stabilized at the annealing temperature and this requires uniformity of temperature; the time of cooling in the high temperature region, t^*, and in the lower temperature region, t_f, depends on the thickness of glass. Thicker glass requires longer time periods and more rigorous control (straight-line cooling and not erratic cooling). Basically, the electric furnace, with temperature controllers, offers more uniform temperatures and more precise control of the annealing temperature and cooling rates than does the gas-fired furnace. It would be preferred for more massive pieces and probably for experimentation or limited production. The electric furnaces are of two major types with respect to heating elements: wire-wound (nichrome or Kanthal) and silicon-carbide rods (Globar or Crystolan). There are many variations in arrangement of heating elements in both types; the carbide-rod type may have the rods mounted vertically or horizontally, for example. Typically, the carbide-rod type will heat from two opposite sides, while the wire-wound type will heat from four sides for a top-loader.

With an increase in the number and size of pieces with each firing, the gas-fired kiln will prove more economical, with the tunnel kiln making loading easy. For limited production or experimentation, it is possible to add glass during the casting process. In such a case one must rebuild the door, usually in the form of a temporary door which is assembled for each firing, with bricks that can be removed so glass can be added to openings in the molds. The calculation of the correct amount of glass was considered in Section 8, under "Preparation of the Glass."

The temperature controller is an important element of the furnace system. One method, a crude one, is to use a temperature indicator—that is to say, a thermocouple with output meter calibrated in degrees centigrade (Celsius) or degrees Fahrenheit which permits one to observe the temperature. One can learn to adjust the controls so as to get reproducible cycles. A second method, which requires an appreciable investment, uses a program controller (costing about $700). This permits changing the cooling rate to adjust for glass thickness for proper annealing.

10. COLORS AND COLORING OF GLASSES

A wide range of colors can be produced in glass. In addition, glasses can be made opalescent, extending the range of colors or effects. We do not propose that compositions be prepared and glass melts made, but that a brief summary of the colorants and their colors be compiled. Such a summary provides a general background which enriches one's understanding of the potential of glass. When one does casting work with colored glasses, some of the colors may change. In particular, the yellows and reds which involve submicroscopic particles may change during reheating to the casting temperature. As the compositions of the commercially colored glasses are not available, it is necessary to build up a general background of data so as to work effectively. Of course, brochures which list colors and corresponding company names are available.

As an example of the range of colors available, Corning Optical Products, of Corning Glass Works, produces glass color filters. They sell a kit of color filters for demonstrating color mixing and light transmission in science classes. Such glasses are made under precise control and would therefore make good reference standards. However, they are expensive and do not match each other in coefficients of expansion. Thus these glasses are not suitable for glassforming.

Catalogs from companies which do sell colored glasses suitable for glassforming will frequently show color photo reproductions. These companies also have sample kits which are available to distributors. The color depends upon the thickness of the sample. The surface of the glass can provide additional effects, for flat glass can be made smooth or textured by special rolls during the drawing process.

When the different compounds that make up the batch are melted together, (see Section 21), they form a fluid solution of oxides which is homogenous. The colorant can be one of three types: (1) ions, of metallic elements like nickel (Ni), cobalt (Co), and chromium (Cr) in solution; (2) atoms, of nonmetallic elements like selenium (Se) in solution; and (3) clusters of atoms or particles of metallic elements like gold (Au) in suspension.

The glass chemistry is extremely complex, as can be seen from a study of the book by W. A. Weyl, *Coloured Glasses* (The Society of Glass Technology, Sheffield, 1951). Dr. Weyl classifies the ionic-solution type into two subclasses; in one the color is due to the ionic environment or surrounding ions, and in the other the color is due to the oxidation state. A shorter summary appears in the book by C. J. Philips, *Glass, the Miracle Maker* (Pitman Publishing Corporation, New York, 1948).

83

The coloring agents and colors are displayed in Table 5, where the three types of colorants are listed, along with the two subclasses of the first type. Some colors depend on various conditions of glass composition and are changed by other constituents like B_2O_3, Na_2O, K_2O, etc. They should be stable upon reheating. Some of these conditions are listed in the table.

TABLE 5:   COLORED GLASSES

	Weyl's Type A: Color Due to Ionic Environment	Weyl's Type B: Color Due to Oxidation State
Group 1: Solution of Ions	NiO colors range from yellow (in glass in B_2O_3 "saturated" environment) to purple (lead silicates) to reddish-violet (potash-lime) to brownish-violet (soda-lime), 1/50,000 produces tint CoO purple (in "saturated" glass) blue (in "unsaturated" glass) 1/500,000 detectable 1/100,000 distinct 1/10,000 intense	CuO neutral or oxidizing green-blue Cr_2O_3 green, aided by As and Sb oxides, acid melt, 1/1000 gives a good color more oxidizing (CrO_3) orange aided by basic melts Ce-TiO_2 yellow Fe_2O_3 yellow FeO blue-green Fe_2O_3-TiO_2 brown Fe_2O_3-MnO_2 amber U_3O_8 yellow U_3O_8-TiO_2 yellow U_3O_8-MnO_2 topaz Fe-C yellow Mn/Ni/Co oxides black Mn/Ni/Co/Cr oxides black
Group 2: Microscopic Particles	Au ruby, 1/50,000 Ag yellow Cu ruby Cu aventurine	
Group 3: Submicroscopic Particles (1) Colored	Selenium reds: Se and CdS and ZnO produce colored particles	
(2) Colorless	Opal, NaF	

Other colors depend on the heat treatment before or during the forming process. When the heat treatment has been an important factor in producing the color, as with the selenium rubies and gold rubies, or in producing an opal phase, then upon reheating to the casting temperature the color may change or the opal phase be altered. For example, some Kokomo yellows and reds, upon reheating for casting, developed yellow and red opals. These changes can be used for design purposes in a constructive way if one is prepared for such changes. On the other hand, to maintain a nice transparent red during casting depends on selection of another composition glass.

Some glass batches are given in the brochure "A Representative Collection of Ceramic Batches" from Ceramic Industry, 5 South Wabash Avenue, Chicago, Illinois 60603, with their colors, but no explanation and no physical properties are shown.

11. GRINDING EQUIPMENT

After a piece has been completed by casting, fusing or other techniques, it may frequently have some region, possibly an edge, that needs finishing Or the piece may be designed so that part is to be removed after forming Such finishing may require use of a diamond wheel cutoff saw, followed by grinding and polishing with a grinding mill.

The iron discs of the grinding mill and laps serve as a vehicle for the abrasive on a trued surface. The abrasive does the actual "cutting" of the glass. Abrasives used are silicon carbide (SiC), aluminum oxide or alumina (Al_2O_3), tin oxide (SnO_2) and cerium oxide (CeO_2). While there is a natural form of aluminum oxide, it is now made synthetically to provide better control of properties; silicon carbide is also made synthetically. Different companies have their trade names for these products. For example, the Norton Company calls aluminum oxide "Alundum" and silicon carbide "Crystolon."

The first step is to choose the proper abrasive for the job. Silicon carbide is used for the rough grinding, aluminum oxide for polishing or finer grinding. Tin oxide and cerium oxide are also used for polishing. The next step is to choose the proper grain size. The numbers designating grain size refer to dimensions of screens used to separate or "size" the abrasive. They represent the number of openings per linear inch in one of the screens. Examples of grain sizes are 10, 12, 14, 16, etc., the larger the number, the finer the abrasive. For example, grain size 30 refers to particles that pass through a screen with 24 openings per inch and are held on the screen with 30 openings per inch.

The table below illustrates grain sizes of Norton abrasives:

TABLE 6:   GRAIN SIZES OF NORTON ABRASIVES

		Coarse to Fine				Flour Sizes	
10	20		70	120		290	
12	24	46	80	150		320	
14	30	54	90	180		400	
16	36	60	100	220		500	
				240		600	

One needs only a few sizes from this list to have a sequence from coarse to fine which permits rough grinding, fine grinding and then polishing. Water is used as a suspension medium for the abrasive and as a coolant. Between operations, as one changes to a finer abrasive, the wheel must be scrupulously cleaned of the coarser abrasive, or the piece will show scratch marks.

The sequence of grinding steps is given in Table 7. In addition to the metal laps, there are also bonded wheels. The abrasive is held by a bond which may be one of several different types: vitrified, resinoid, rubber, shellac, and silicate. There are different-sized abrasives and different ratios of abrasive to bonding material. "Grade" refers to the wheel's hardness. "Structure" refers to the proportion and arrangement of the abrasive and bond. Many excellent brochures on abrasives and grinding wheels are available from the Norton Company.

TABLE 7:   GRINDING SEQUENCE

Step	Abrasive
1	70 Crystolon
2	120 Alundum
3	220 Alundum
4	Optical Flour (Medium)
5	Rouge

Some remarks should be made on grinding techniques. The grinding method is called "freehand" or "offhand" as no jigs or fixtures are used and the piece is held in the hands. A dry wheel can "grab" the glass and pull it out of the hands, so the wheel must be kept wet and covered with abrasive. This may be done by periodic sprinkling with water, which spins out and off the edge, and then sprinkling on abrasive. Or one may do it continuously, using a can with some kind of a stopcock for dripping water into a trough filled with abrasive. Water and abrasive drip down onto the wheel. When water and abrasive are on the wheel, the glass is held firmly in both hands and lowered onto the wheel, then pressed down. The leading edge grinds fastest; one must be alert to maintain the ground surface parallel to the planned surface. Both the leading edge and the trailing edge can be chipped quite easily when lowering the glass onto the mill surface. The piece can be turned around so the trailing edge becomes the leading edge, to aid in keeping alignment with the planned surface. It is easy to develop a curved surface or two flat surfaces at slightly different angles instead of a single surface.

12. ACID ETCHING

There is a glass-finishing technique which can alter the surface of the glass object either uniformly overall or in selected areas. The surface may be made to have a translucent effect or polished. This technique, in the broad sense, is called "acid etching": it refers to the chemical corrosion of the glass surface.

If the acid treatment produces a brilliant, smooth surface, it is called "acid polishing." If the surface has a shiny, satiny appearance, it has had "satin etch." If the surface is more dull and lifeless, and translucent, it has had "matte etch." These last two techniques are called by the more general term of "frosting." Thus we see that etching of glass includes both polishing and frosting.

The major chemicals to carry out this technique are acid fluorides. They are hydrofluoric acid and double salts of hydrofluoric acid such as ammonium bifluoride, sodium bifluoride, etc. In aqueous solution, the bifluorides release hydrofluoric acid, so they have the same effects as does hydrofluoric acid in many applications.

The acid fluorides are of major safety concern in industry or workshops because of their potential for causing serious and aggravating burns, which are painful and slow to heal. When working around hydrofluoric acid one should adopt the attitude that anything which is wet is acid, not just water. When concentrated acid strikes, one is aware of a burn in a few minutes, but dilute acid—as low as 0.5 percent—can cause a delayed burn which will not be known for hours, when it has become deep-seated. Gloves must be used, and they must be of industrial rubber, not just the household type. The gloves must be checked periodically for pinholes.

There are excellent brochures on hydrofluoric acid and safety precautions from The Harshaw Chemical Company, the Du Pont Company, and the Allied Chemical Company. A basic safety brochure is available from the Manufacturing Chemists Association, 1825 Connecticut Avenue, N.W., Washington, D.C. 20009.

The solubility of glasses in acids depends upon the glass composition, the acid etching bath composition, and the temperature. Most compositions are appreciably attacked by hydrofluoric acid, and the rate of attack increases as the temperature is raised. Avoid higher temperatures as they are less convenient and acid is lost by volatilization as the temperature is raised. Acid fumes are noxious, can cause considerable discomfort and possibly harmful effects. The concentrated acid used to prepare the acid baths is a highly fuming material.

The acid bath is prepared by diluting concentrated acid with water or small quantities of sulfuric, hydrochloric, or nitric acid. Typical procedures are as follows: The object is first cleaned in a bath of 100 parts water, 12 parts concentrated sulfuric acid, and 1 part concentrated hydrochloric acid. (Caution! Always prepare acid solutions by adding the acid to water slowly, as much heat is produced and local boiling and splattering of acid can take place.) Place the object in wire or plastic cage, dip for eighty seconds, with four dips of twenty seconds each preferred. Wash the object well, using long-sleeved rubber gloves, and dry in an acid-free room.

The object is then dipped in the polishing bath, which is contained in a lead-lined steel tank, a rubber-lined steel tank, or a polyethylene or unplasticized polyvinyl tank. The polishing bath is made up as follows:

Bath Composition	For Lime Glass	For Lead Glass
Strong Hydrofluoric Acid (70–80%)	6 parts	3 parts
Strong Sulfuric Acid (92–98%)	7 parts	2 parts
Water	3–4 parts	1 part

The mixture is preferably kept at 50°C, but in the small workshop, it is more convenient to work at room temperature. If at 50°C, a dip of thirty seconds gives a polish. If there is no etching at all, even with longer dips, a higher proportion of hydrofluoric acid is required. If the etching is too matte, then add more water. If a matte etching is desired, one needs more hydrofluoric acid in the above mixture.

Other bath compositions are available, usually with some of the bifluorides added. The Harshaw Chemical Company has a brochure on glass frosting and polishing which gives other compositions. It is a very useful brochure because it tells about the design and construction of equipment: tanks, tank ventilating system, drainboards, baskets, and rinsing and drying equipment.

In the polishing procedure, after dipping, rinse well with water, then brush. Glasses show uniform etching properties if they are homogenous. However, slight variations in composition can affect the etching and the final appearance of the cast pieces.

One may wish to achieve different depths of etching by using acid resists. The resist can be a wax resist or a commercial photosensitive-type resist. If wax, it is applied uniformly and thinly, and then a desired design can be cut through to the glass surface. If one wants to etch deeply, then periodic rinsing is required to remove the white residue left by the chemical action of the acid on the glass. If this is not done, then the object will be etched unevenly. It may be necessary to retouch the resist several times to prevent undercutting during deep etching. The cast piece by Decorchemont (Figure 37) was acid-etched using a resist, and a delicate pattern is achieved over the whole surface.

There is a serious problem on disposal of wastes to comply with local regulations, either for stream pollution or for sewage disposal. Neutralization with lime will result in effluents with the lowest amount of soluble fluorides in them. The Harshaw Chemical Company brochure and the Manufacturing Chemists Association brochure discuss disposal of wastes.

The whole area of acid etching of glass may be explored, not by setting up an etching room in the workshop, but by turning to a commercial company prepared to work with the craftsman. Such a company might be a chemical laboratory or a company working in art glass. The latter are found in most major cities. Following the preliminary work, one could set out to refine the artistic aspects.

Part Four | Design

13. INTRODUCTION

The world of art and decorative art is an ever-changing one, modified and influenced by technological advances in all periods. Once such a technical advance becomes accepted, the artist or craftsman has simply another tool at his disposal, and then all the emphasis can be placed on the artistic and design aspects. From the study of the history of art and of technology, one can enumerate technical achievements which permitted the creation of new fine arts or new decorative arts—oil painting, etching, lithography, photography for example. Recent changes have been made in older techniques, like metalworking. There, gas and arc welding are new technical developments which now are accepted artistic and decorative-art techniques.

Even woodworking techniques have had their evolution, and one step, in Japan, is documented:

> "And the sculptor Unkei . . . was as great an innovator as the warriors and philosophers who employed him. His name sounds in Japanese ears as the name of Michelangelo sounds in our own . . . It is, therefore, to be expected that Unkei, like the great artists of every age, was deeply concerned with techniques. He is credited with inventing an entirely new system of joinery to make his figures. Perhaps its greatest use was to set free the mind of the sculptor from the restrictions of shape imposed by the log and plank and block."
>
> *Warner, L.,* The Enduring Art of Japan,
> *Harvard University Press, Cambridge, 1952, page 45*

Glassmaking has had its many innovations in the past, as was mentioned in Part One. Take a very modest example—that of cutting glass. Theophilus, in Book II, Chapter XVIII, "Cutting the Glass," and Chapter

XXIX, "Simple Windows," tells about cutting glass by touching it with a hot iron "cutting tool" and trimming the edge with a "groesing iron." The first procedure breaks the glass by "heat shock" in an irregular and erratic manner. The description does not reveal working procedures accurately, but without a doubt the simple steel or tungsten-carbide wheel cutter we use today is a dramatic improvement, giving a precision of cutting undreamed of in Theophilus's time. It can "set free the mind of the sculptor" from limitations imposed by irregular edges and can make possible precise fitting of glass against glass, without leads, in designs analogous to "hard-edge" painting.

Another recent innovation, associated with glassmaking for combining and sealing glasses, is cementing with clear epoxies. This can "set free the mind of the sculptor" from limitations imposed by physical properties of diverse glasses and opens up all kinds of possibilities of new "stained" glass window designs and glass built up to great thickness in three-dimensional patterns.

Our studies of the history of glassmaking techniques reveal how difficult it is to introduce a really new technique that is worthy of the effort. However, it is clear that there are some *ideas* or *concepts* well worth examining. First, the concept that glassmaking *can be simple* is very important. This simplicity is clearly revealed if one starts with flameworking, then glassforming as described in this book, and finally glassblowing. Then the progression is a series of modest sequential steps.

Even within a single technique there can be incremental steps. Our own experience with flameworking has been an awareness of only *simple changes*, but when one compares present work with work of three years ago, for example, there are dramatic differences.

Second, there are valuable concepts about glass properties: the transparent-metal analogy, the high-temperature viscous-liquid property, and the low-temperature solid property. Familiarity with these concepts gives artists, craftsmen, and designers an understanding of the material which will permit the exploration of the design potential of glass using the most advantageous technique.

Third, the artist may use new materials. For example, the use of transparent epoxies for sealing glass to glass bypasses the limitations of physical properties, both the expansion mismatch and annealing difficulties, so that this compromise adds new simplicity to glassforming.

If we turn now to glassforming techniques, we see that the three methods—sagging and laminating, mold-fusing, and mold-casting—permit an increasing complexity of shapes. That is why we have chosen to present the work in this order. Sagging, basically, starts with a flat sheet, or a bottle, or some similar commercially available shape, and gives it a rather gentle or shallow curve. Mold-fusing, the next stage, permits the fusing together of glass arranged in a mold. The arrangement is built up of small sections of glass, usually standing perpendicular to the surface of the mold rather than in layers. The arrangement of glass that is not likely to collapse during assembly is the mold shape having a shallow bowl-like design, while the shape that has almost vertical walls requires some care in assembly. Therefore the basic design is an open bowl-like shape. Mold-casting, on the other hand, gives much more freedom of design, ranging from plaques or reliefs to sculpture and hollow designs. The latter has the limitations of metal casting, and one should design the mold so as to have the most convenient arrangement for supporting the interior cores and for the addition of glass.

14. LAMINATING AND ENAMELS AS PAINTINGS

The starting point for most workers using laminating, with or without enamels (glass colors), would be to make small things like ashtrays and ornaments. We think that the real excitement lies in the vision of large areas of glass having a painting quality, a very special painting quality, with vibrant color and a luminosity by transmitted light which no conventional painting can achieve. Working with laminating only, one may use a collage technique (see H. Janis and R. Blesh, *Collage*, Chilton Book Company, Philadelphia, 1969), although with a "harder" edge than if one has used papers with long fibers and torn them. Working with enamels, and glass colors, one may use a painting technique in a wide range of styles. The colors themselves may range from transparent to opaque. One can laminate pieces to build up surface textures, as with impasto. By laminating very thickly, one may achieve a three-dimensional effect which is unique because of the transparent medium.

Progress in this field has actually been very slow. It may well be that exposure to conventional stained-glass windows since childhood has prevented many people from seeing the potential. But we have met several artists who have fallen so in love with the colors of glass that they have decided they *must* work in glass. They have then proceeded to do so, overcoming many technical difficulties.

15. SAGGING FOR ASSEMBLAGES

The starting and finishing point, for most workers doing sagging, is to collapse bottles for ashtrays or, more recently, to elongate bottles in a kind of pop-art concept. We think that there is a more exciting vision in making an assemblage.

We are not suggesting that the final result will be profound, but that there is excitement in the designing, the seeking out of suitable starting shapes, the cutting of the glass, the designing of molds so that the glass can be sagged into or draped over the mold, depending on the design concept, and then the final assembling. Likewise there is an excitement in discovering shapes which in themselves suggest designs, and in the use of color.

This work direction is possible only through the use of epoxy cements. To fuse the glasses would require molds of great complexity. We suggest one reason that this area has not been investigated is the reluctance of experts to mix materials. But the epoxy cements permit easy sealing of glass to glass. They even suggest combining glass with wood and metal. At this stage, there are almost no technical difficulties—the designer's mind has been set free from restrictions.

An example of the assemblage technique is the work of Robert W. Brown, shown earlier in Color Plate 9, with detail in Color Plate 10.

16. CASTING SHAPES

There is a variety of shapes that can be made by casting glass, just as in the case of metal. Of course, transparency will make a basic difference in design concept.

RELIEFS

The simplest procedure and design concept characterize the relief. The modeling of the clay is done directly in a very natural manner, building up or carving away, keeping in mind that the glass will duplicate the object. Several examples have already been shown; the results of modeling the surface with cut places and textures is much more dramatic in glass, when properly lighted, than in clay.

A wide variety of designs and patterns is possible. Briefly, they might be classified as freehand designs and designs drawn with mechanical methods, as with straightedge and French curves. Fine lines and fine points, relief or intaglio, present difficulties in creating in clay, in being reproduced in the mold material without breaking, and finally in getting a good casting in glass. Rather, bold designs, with boldly modeled planes and surfaces, are the most successful.

The freehand patterns can be stamped lines, patterns of points, regular, irregular, interrupted, circular, broken, unbroken and other line patterns. A source which illustrates many such patterns is a book by Ernst Röttger and Dieter Klante, *Creative Drawing* (Reinhold Book Corporation, New York, 1963). Scripts and monograms make another interesting and successful variation. Sources which are very suggestive are Donald M. Anderson, *The Art of Written Forms* (Holt, Rinehart and Winston, New York, 1969), and Rudolph Koch, *The Book of Signs* (Dover Publications, Inc., New York). If one experiments with novel arrangements of letters or characters, the book edited by Emmett Williams, *An Anthology of Concrete Poetry* (Something Else Press, New York, 1967), suggests many visual patterns of letters and words.

INTAGLIO

The rear surface of the casting is flat and transparent. Upon looking at a relief through the rear, one may discover a new design, sometimes quite satisfying. The design can be improved for viewing through the rear surface by making it in intaglio. If one has the ability, the original clay model could be made directly to produce the rear-surface intaglio; otherwise the model can be made in relief, a first casting can be made in plaster, and then a second one off that in the plaster-silica mixture.

Sculpture

Sculptural shapes, with sharp edges and strong textures, can be cast. The basic limitation is one of wall thickness or massiveness, for that affects the annealing step. This will be discussed further in the next section and in Appendix 2. From a design point of view, the viscous-liquid property during casting and the flow patterns produced with colors as a result of this property should be considered carefully. Equally important is the transparency, which can grade into translucency or even opaqueness, depending on the composition. The transparency is usually disturbing in realistic sculpture, but may prove to be exciting in abstract or nonobjective sculpture or decorative art. Then the optical effects and surface treatment which will be mentioned below can be used to enhance the design.

There is an unending variety of natural shapes and forms, or modifications of such, as starting points for glass sculpture. Shapes like stones and bones, stylized crystals, polished jewels, and seashells are only a few.

Flow Patterns

The *viscous-liquid property* of glass during the casting process permits colored flow patterns to be set up if one starts with small bits of clear and colored glass. As the temperature is raised, these bits soften and flow down under the action of gravity to fill the mold. There is no homogenizing action; rather the bits elongate and seal together as "striae," giving a pleasing and subtle effect which cannot be obtained by any other mixing technique used in glassmaking. For example, on flowing down, the striae can fold over on the bottom. Mixing of glasses can be done at the marver table for free-blowing, but the results are different.

For casting, the patterns cannot be designed and are accidental in nature, but the colors, the amounts of transparent and colored glass, the sizes of the bits added and the preliminary arrangement in the reservoir above the mold are all conscious design decisions. The design potential of "frozen-in" flow patterns of colored glass, or opalescent and clear glasses, is really unexplored. For example, no one has made duplications of one design with variations of the amounts of transparent and colored glasses—a kind of experiment someone who has made glaze studies would do most naturally. Out of such experiments new control of the process could be achieved.

Internal Interfaces

It is even possible to get striae in clear glass. Such striae are visible when two clear glasses of different refractive index are mixed. When glasses are mixed, it is important that they have the same coefficients of expansion (see Appendix 1), so that stress is not set up at the interfaces between the different glasses after cooling. Glasses with matching coefficients of expansion have been developed deliberately and are available commercially for combining colored glasses, but for clear glasses they have not been so developed. However, a wide range of refractive index glasses have been made for optical elements and the choice is so great that it is possible to find some that have matching coefficients of expansion.

17. SURFACE EFFECTS

OPTICAL DESIGN

Using the *transparent property* and the *solid property*, one can proceed to design glass shapes which will have interesting optical effects. These effects depend on refraction or bending of light rays at the surface. The surfaces may have prism-like or lens-like properties, and of course, nearby surfaces can be related in some complementary manner, or the interior surface of a hollow object may act as a single large lens, with the surroundings imaged by this lens, or small lenses might be designed in one surface and the image of another surface seen reduced in size in each lens. Such techniques were used in the design of American cut glass, although the patterns are so intricate that one sees the faceted surfaces and not the imaging properties of these surfaces. There was an experimental design show of Steuben Glass, about 1955, which stressed prismatic effects, and various pieces designed since then have emphasized the imaging properties of the surfaces.

SURFACE TREATMENT

The surface texture is also important for the design. Flameworked and free-blown glasses have extremely smooth surfaces, while sagged glass may be very smooth, and mold-cast glass may have a matte surface where the glass contacted the mold, a smooth surface if there was no contact. The surfaces can be roughened further or polished by lapidary techniques, using grinding and polishing wheels (see Section 11), or they can be acid-polished (see Section 12).

18. LIMITATIONS

In flameworking and glassblowing limitations arise from the processes used, which involve rotation. Thus the basic forms all have axial symmetry. Of course, such forms can be distorted by twisting and folding and pulling. Smooth surfaces and rounded edges are produced as a result of the viscous-liquid property of glass at high temperature and as a result of the surface-tension property (a property of liquids). Therefore, as a limitation, one cannot make sharp edges and rough surfaces.

In contrast, fusing and casting seem less limiting. Complex shapes can be built up in laminating, and rough surfaces, sharp edges, and sharp indentations can be formed by casting, so that there is great freedom of design. The main limitation is the thickness of a single piece, cast or fused. If the piece is too thick, the annealing process will have to be carried out with great care in a special furnace with programmed cooling. Under such conditions pieces several inches thick can be annealed relatively free of stress. One other limitation of the glassforming processes is that the smooth, rounded surfaces of free-blowing and flameworking cannot be made.

19. UNIQUENESS

The transparency, the range of colors, the shading from transparent to translucent (or opalescent) to opaque, and the techniques of glassmaking—all these combine to make glass a unique material. And it is the combination of these factors, rather than any one, that makes glass unique. As has been mentioned in the introduction, the techniques of flameworking and free-blowing are the most exciting and dramatic because the craftsman works in a relatively direct manner. These techniques remain unique among the crafts. The glassforming techniques are indirect—one assembles or builds up a laminated shape or makes a model for casting. The casting and fusing techniques produce forms which cannot be duplicated by flameworking or free-blowing, forms with sharp edges and a variety of surface textures. Unusual flow patterns and optical effects all add to the design potential of glass.

Part Five | The Story of the Glassformer's Material

20. INTRODUCTION: MANUFACTURE OF GLASS IN THE SMALL FACTORY

While the craftsman who works with sheet glass, cullet, or glass marbles need never know how his glass is prepared, or what the constituents are that make up his glasses, it is very desirable that some basic information be made easily available to him. He is then better prepared to use both chemical and physical knowledge to work with colored glass and to understand differences in working properties and annealing temperatures of glasses, no matter what process he uses. When he uses untested scrap glass from a junkyard and his work cracks upon cooling, he will not be surprised. For the person who has done only laminating or sagging or casting, this discussion will open new horizons should he have the chance to visit a glass factory in America or Europe.

Large production factories are usually noisily dramatic, but it is the small glass factory with hand-shop operations which is exciting. There the operations, requiring such wonderful skill and coordination, can be seen clearly and easily. There are, of course, hidden details—the preparation of the glass batch and melting. Details of the steps to prepare, melt, and work glass are described below. In some of the small colored sheet glass factories, the operations of ladling glass into the rolling machine and the rolling of the sheet can be observed.

21. METHODS AND TECHNIQUES

Oxide Composition of the Glass

One begins in the factory with the composition of the glass (or glasses) to be melted. Glasses are mixtures of oxides. The basic composition can be expressed in terms of weight percentages of those oxides. For example, a base glass could be a "lead" glass, one containing lead oxide. Such artistic glass may contain about 30–36 percent lead oxide (PbO), 10–13 percent potassium oxide (K_2O), and 53–56 percent silica (SiO_2). One must consider some specific composition, like the following:

Lead oxide	PbO	30%
Potassium oxide	K_2O	15
Silica	SiO_2	55
Total		100%

A second composition to consider is that of window glass or bottle glass. These soda-lime (or lime) glasses are made from inexpensive raw materials, have good working properties, and are used when high heat resistance and chemical stability are not required. A typical composition is:

Sodium oxide	Na_2O	15%
Calcium oxide (lime)	CaO	9
Magnesium oxide	MgO	3
Aluminum oxide	Al_2O_3	1
Silica	SiO_2	72
Total		100%

This is also the composition representative of the colored sheet glasses commercially available.

For purposes of comparison, a high-softening-temperature borosilicate glass is composed of:

Sodium oxide	Na_2O	3.8%
Potassium oxide	K_2O	0.4
Boric oxide	B_2O_3	12.9
Aluminum oxide	Al_2O_3	2.2
Silica	SiO_2	80.7
Total		100.0%

This so-called "hard" glass is the one commonly used in scientific flameworking, and its low coefficient of thermal expansion is a decided advantage (see Section 4). This is the glass which we have recommended and continue to recommend for artistic flameworking.

A fourth type, of interest for some of the university or college workshops, is a special "soft" glass containing boric oxide and used for making fiber glass commercially, but remelted in the workshops from either cullet or glass marbles.

COLORS

To the above glasses, for example the lead oxide, which is clear and called "crystal," or the soda-lime glass, which is also clear, one may add certain materials to produce colors. They are mostly oxides, like cobalt oxide, iron oxide, uranium oxide, although yellows and reds are produced by sulfur and selenium compounds. Other ingredients produce translucent glass ("opals") which affect the color quality very much. Colors were discussed in Section 10.

Certain physical properties (see Appendix 1: "Expansion Coefficient," "Annealing Point," "Softening Point") will change with the addition of moderate amounts of these materials so that some adjustment of the initial composition may be necessary to maintain a given physical property. If the expansion coefficient is decreased by the addition of these materials, then more alkali, which increases the expansion coefficient, can be added.

BATCH COMPOSITION AND RAW MATERIALS

The next step is to convert the above formulas by weights of oxides into weights of raw materials to be used on some arbitrary scale of batch. That is, the oxides may be supplied by some more complex material. Many raw materials may be used in glassmaking, but their ultimate function is to furnish the oxides which will remain after they decompose—oxides as listed in the compositions, like silica (SiO_2), potassium oxide (K_2O), lead oxide (PbO), boric oxide (B_2O_3), aluminum oxide (Al_2O_3), and sodium oxide (Na_2O). As a specific example, potassium carbonate (K_2CO_3) may yield the potassium oxide (K_2O) after the melting process has taken place and carbon dioxide (CO_2) has been evolved. The oxides have different functions, with SiO_2 playing the key role, that of the "glassformer." A book on glass manufacture will give a list of various raw materials, with the common name of each, its scientific name, chemical formula, the oxide yielded after decomposition, and the weight percentage of the oxide yielded. The weight percentage of oxide yielded from the raw material is known by chemical analysis (for example, pearl ash yields 57 percent potassium oxide), and thus the amount of raw materials can be calculated to give the desired weight of glass. For example:

Lead oxide	Pb_3O_4	26.9%
Pearl ash	$K_2CO_3 \cdot 3/2H_2O$	15.4
Potassium nitrate	KNO_3	9.4
Silica	SiO_2	48.2
Total		99.9%

is similar to the lead oxide base glass composition presented above.

Furnaces, Glass-Melting Pots, and Glassmaking Tools

There are three types of glass-melting furnaces, each attempting to meet a different need. It will be seen that they are not strictly comparable. "Pot" furnaces vary in size and hold from one to sixteen ceramic containers, called "pots." If more than one pot is used, then different-colored glasses can be melted at the same time, which is a requirement for most artistic-glass production. The second type, the "day tank," is a batch melting furnace. Most of the furnaces used in the universities or colleges are small day tanks. The third type, used in large factory production, is the "continuous tank." As its name suggests, it has raw materials entering at one end periodically and melted glass removed continuously at the other end to make bottles, sheet glass, tubing, television tube face plates, etc. In the day tank and the continuous tank, the refractory walls also serve as the walls of the container to hold the molten glass. Only one color at a time can be melted in those units. They usually hold more glass than does a single pot.

A crucible, which is really a small pot, may hold as little as a fraction of a pound, while a large pot may hold as much as 3000 pounds of glass. Day tanks may hold from pounds to several tons of glass. Continuous tanks may hold several hundred pounds to several hundred tons and may yield from pounds per hour to tons per hour.

There are a number of tools used in the small factory for the operation of a pot furnace or day tank. There is a large fork mounted on wheels for moving the heavy pots out of the furnace. There are ladles and rakes for cleaning the surface of the glass, or for removing the glass at the bottom of an almost empty pot. Such glass cannot be utilized and must be removed prior to refilling with batch. There are ladles for dipping out glass to carry to the rolling machine in the small sheet-glass factory.

Glassmaking Operations

For working the glass only a few tools are used now just as in ancient times when blowing was invented. The blowiron is used to "gather" the glass out of the pot or tank. The blowiron is a long hollow iron tube, about four feet in length. The workman holds it by one end and dips the other end—which has a slightly enlarged "nose"—into the glass. He rotates the iron and winds up a gob, or gather, of glass. Later he inflates the glass by blowing into the mouthpiece. Other procedures could be carried out with an additional blowiron, but customarily another tool is used instead, the punty (French *pontil*). This is a solid iron rod, also about four feet long, which costs somewhat less than the hollow iron. It was probably developed simply because it was cheaper. With the punty the workman gathers glass and applies it or "lays" it onto a blown shape. The punty, with a small amount of glass at the tip, may be attached or sealed to the bottom of a blown vessel on the blow-iron, and the vessel may then be severed or "cracked off" the blowiron.

There are tools for controlling the shape of the gather before blowing, and for altering the shape during the blowing process. They are the marver, forming block, board, wood jack, and shears (see Figure 100).

The gather at the end of the blowiron is rolled or "marvered" on the marver table, a polished iron slab. This marvering shapes the gather into a cylindrical form and chills the surface (see Figures 101 through 103). If a spherical form is desired, then the gather is rotated in a wetted wooden block having a hollowed hemispherical form. Such an operation is called "block-ing." If the glass is sufficiently hot so that it flows easily, cooling the surface with water prevents any stresses, the glass will not crack, and the water is turned to steam. This also chills the surface, an operation which gives con-trol during the inflation step.

After the preliminary shaping, the gather can be inflated. The shape is controlled by rubbing with a wooden board (the worker sits in the "chair") and by the pincers or wood jack, along with rotation of the vessel by rolling the blowiron on the arms of the chair.[8] In addition, the action of gravity stretches the hot glass if it hangs down, or flattens it if it is held upright. The wood jack is a pincers with wooden tips.

After the vessel is blown to size the punty is attached directly opposite the blowiron nose, at what will become the base, and the glass severed from the blowiron by chilling it there and striking the iron a blow with a metal rod. The glass is reheated and the opening, where the blowiron had been attached, is enlarged and cut down with a shears (amazingly enough!) The shape may be spun out into a disk if desired, by centrifugal force. It is shaped by using the board and wood jack (pincers).

The process of shaping the glass takes some time so that it cools while being worked, becoming less fluid until it can no longer be deformed. Therefore reheating is done periodically by inserting the glass, and of course the tip of the iron, into the furnace opening at the pot or day tank or into a special reheating furnace called the "glory hole." Use of the separate reheat-ing furnace is the common practice now. The handle of the iron may become too hot to hold and water may have to be sprayed onto it. More important, the point where the glass is sealed to the iron should not become too hot, as the whole vessel may fall or flow right off the iron; if the iron becomes too cold the piece may crack off.

Customarily there are five men who work together in a group or team called a "shop." The "gaffer" is the master glassblower, who sits in the wooden chair (see Figure 104), which has two elongated arms. He rotates the blowiron or punty on these arms during the shaping of the article. As he rotates the iron he applies the various tools described (the board, wood jack,

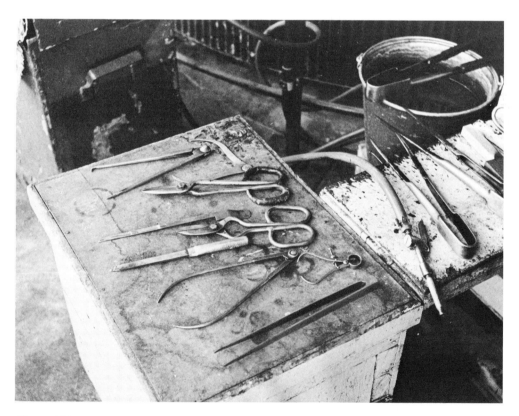

Figure 100. *Glassblowing tools.*

and forming block) or uses the shears to trim off some glass (rotating more slowly at the same time that he is cutting glass. The "servitor," his chief assistant, makes the initial gather and does the preliminary shaping at the marver table. The "blower" is the second assistant who carries the piece one step farther before handing it to the gaffer. Thus considerable work may be done on the object before the gaffer actually takes over. The "bit-gatherer" gathers small gobs of glass for application of handles, legs, feet, knobs, etc. He holds the iron with the glass close to the object. The gaffer, seated in the chair, seizes the glass with a special shears and guides it into position above the object, which he also controls and rotates as necessary, combining both actions during application of the glass and then shearing it off. The "taker-in" is the fifth member of the team—he carries the finished article(s) to a furnace, called a "lehr," for controlled cooling.

The controlled cooling process, called annealing, is the last step in glass-making. After the object is completed, it must be held for a while at the "annealing temperature," or "annealing point," even reheating to that temperature if necessary. After the holding period it is cooled gradually. If the cooling is done properly, the stresses in the glass are reduced to a minimum and it is less likely to break. Annealing is discussed in greater detail in Appendix 2.

Preparation of Enamels and Glass Colors

Enamels and glass colors can be prepared by ladling the glass into water, where it cracks into smaller pieces because of heat shock. Then it can be ground to a finer size, as desired for the particular application.

Preparation of Glass for Mold-Casting or Mold-Fusion

Glass may be ladled out onto a metal casting table, rolled to some convenient thickness with a metal roller, much like rolling bread dough, and, after some cooling to become more rigid, transferred to an annealing furnace. Such a method was used in the past to prepare glass that would become "plate glass."

Other methods, like ladling into water where the glass is chilled quickly and breaks into small pieces, or ladling into a marble-making machine, where it ends up as uniform round marbles, can be used.

Preparation of Patterned Canes for Mold-Fusion

The nineteenth-century technique of constructing patterned canes, called "filigree" canes, requires that one assemble the basic pattern from a group of canes, each of a single type or color; thus these canes must be made first. The steps describing this and the remainder of the operation are as follows:

Figure 101. *Gathering.*

Figure 102. *Marvering.*

Figure 103. *Shaping glass.*

1. One gathers glass from a pot on a punty rod, marvers true and then rams it into a slightly tapered mold of triangular, square, hexagonal or circular cross section, open at the bottom. It is then lifted out and reheated and then stretched, either by attaching another punty and having two men pull, or by seizing the end with a tongs and pulling. In the latter case, it is stretched only a few feet, broken off, reheated and pulled out a few feet again. The canes now have the same cross section as the mold, only reduced. A good size with which to work is about ¼ inch in diameter and 6 inches long, so the longer ones can be cut to this length. Incidentally, a 4-inch-diameter cylindrical shape stretched to a cane of ¼-inch diameter would be 256 times as long as at the start.
2. Now the 6-inch lengths of these canes are arranged in a pattern, making use of the different colors to achieve the desired effect. If the bundle is about 3 inches in diameter, then about 140 canes would be used. For greater detail of the pattern, more canes with smaller diameter could be used. The bundle is wrapped with iron wire (see Figure 105), placed on a brick, and then heated slowly at the furnace. It is pushed forward slowly until one end is hot and fused together.
3. Then it is picked up with a tongs, and the hot end is placed on a shaped hot gob on a punty in a vertical position (see Figure 106).
4. The iron wires are cut off, and the bundle is heated again, then marvered carefully to make it cohere. This is done from the rear, where it is attached to the punty, toward the front in such a way as to force out the air (Figure 107).
5. If desired, the bundle is then dipped into a pot of glass, covered with a layer of another color, and marvered.
6. After reheating, another punty is attached to the free end (Figure 108). Two men can then pull and elongate the glass until it is a cane about ¼ inch in diameter, just as in the original cane-forming operation. The pattern runs lengthwise and is reduced in size (Figure 109). Of course, it need not be reduced so much in size.

The marvelous ancient miniature mosaics, discussed in Section 3, and illustrated in Figures 29, 30, and 31, must have had a similar elongation step and therefore a reduction in size. While the nineteenth-century technique is a known one, the ancient Egyptian process is only speculative.

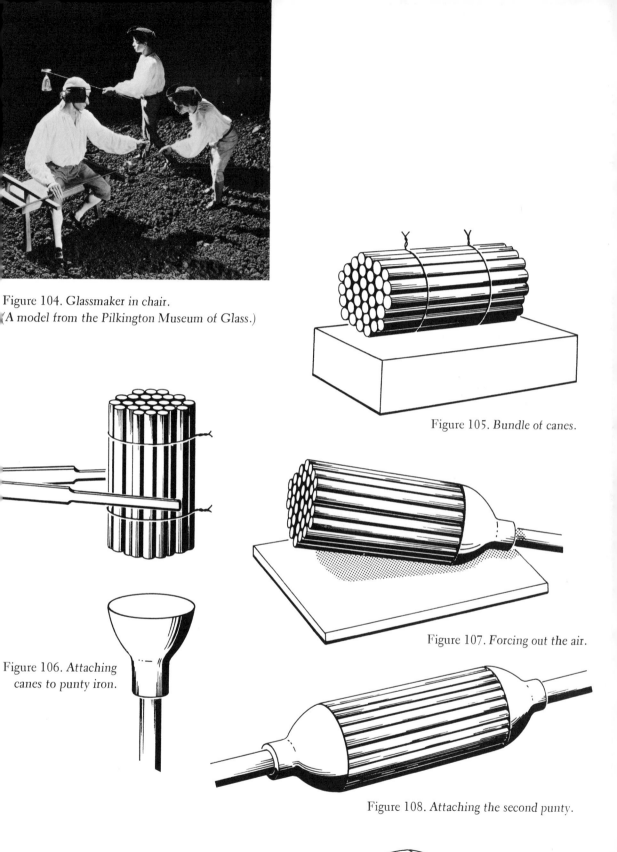

Figure 104. Glassmaker in chair.
(A model from the Pilkington Museum of Glass.)

Figure 105. Bundle of canes.

Figure 106. Attaching
canes to punty iron.

Figure 107. Forcing out the air.

Figure 108. Attaching the second punty.

Figure 109. Stretching the cane.

22. MANUFACTURE OF SHEET GLASS FOR SAGGING AND LAMINATING

OLD METHODS

Crown and Cylinder

The sheet glass is the starting material for sagging and laminating, and is one of the glass forms used for enameling. The hand-shop methods were the "cylinder" method and the "crown" method. The cylinder method, mentioned in Section 5, involves blowing a cylinder, cracking off both ends, and cracking down a side. It is placed in a flattening furnace and if the crack is uppermost the glass will sag with an unrolling motion and end up flat. The method was used in the time of Theophilus and is described in his book *The Various Arts*. By the nineteenth century, very large cylinders were made in the factory by hand. In 1903, the Lubbers process semimechanically made the cylinders 40 feet long, and the splitting and flattening were done as before.

The crown method is very old also. It involves blowing a large bulb, attaching the punty opposite the blowiron, severing the bulb from the blowiron, reheating the bulb, spinning it out into a flat disk (see Figure 110), severing the disk from the punty, and finally annealing. The flat disk is thickened in the center (the "bull's-eye"). Some of the old houses in Boston, on Beacon Hill, have the bull's-eyes in the glass over the front door.

Hand Shop: Ladling and Rolling

In the small glass factory specializing in flat colored sheet, glass is removed from the glass melting pot in a ladle and poured on top of two rolls. This is then rolled out into a flat piece of somewhat irregular shape, which must be trimmed to some standard size.

Casting plate glass on a table, with a roll that squeezed the glass thin, the roll itself being supported by two rails, one at each side, was a late eighteenth-century invention. Then, in 1845, a rolling machine with two rolls was invented. As above, the glass was added on top of the two rolls with a ladle. This was the precursor to the continuous processes described in the next section.

MODERN LARGE-FACTORY METHODS

Historical Remarks

The Lubbers window-glass machine and the Owens bottle machine, both introduced at about the same time, were the first steps in mechanizing the glass industry. One of the faults of the cylinder method was that the flat-

112

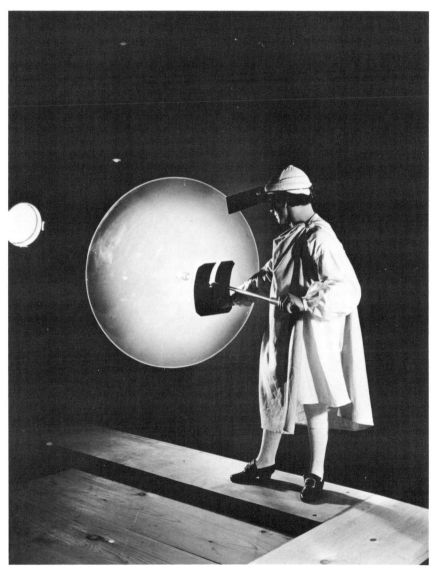

Figure 110. *The crown method. (Pilkington Museum of Glass)*

tened glass had waves in it. Much energy was devoted in America and Europe to the invention of continuous processes which would produce flat glass free of waves. The Colburn machine was introduced in 1917; the Fourcault process was introduced into the United States in 1923. At about this time the Pittsburgh Plate Glass Co. developed a third continuous process. These processes are described below.

Fourcault Process

In the Fourcault process (Figure 111), used by American St. Gobain Corp., the sheet form is generated by glass flowing through a slot in a ceramic material, called a "debiteuse." It is a sculptured ceramic, lighter than the glass, which in section appears as an inverted "V" with the slot aperture upward at the narrow end of the "V." There is a shallow rim surrounding the top perimeter. To produce a flow of glass through the slot, the debiteuse is depressed approximately one inch, so that hydrostatic pressure extrudes glass through this slot, while the rim prevents flooding from above. At the same time the debiteuse is depressed, the glass is engaged by a metal "bait," which pulls it upward with a continuous ribbon of glass following until asbestos rolls contact the glass and continue to elevate it.

The slot is symmetrical and both surfaces are contacted by rolls. The glass at this point is supposed to be sufficiently rigid so that the rolls do not mar the surface.

Colburn Process

In the Colburn process (Figure 112), used by Libbey-Owens-Ford, the ribbon is drawn upward freely from the surface of the glass, then passes over a bending roll about two feet above the bath and moves horizontally through a heated tunnel where it undergoes controlled cooling. The bending roll is a nonoxidizing alloy and highly polished. During the free drawing of the ribbon of glass, the width of the ribbon tends to narrow because of surface-tension forces. This effect is offset by the use of driven knurled stub rolls which touch a few outer inches of the ribbon, and as the stub rolls are water-cooled, they chill the edge sufficiently to control the width of the ribbon.

The process is unsymmetrical; one surface of the glass never contacts the drawing roll, nor does it touch rolls in the annealing lehr.

Pennvernon Process

The Pennvernon process (Figure 113), used by PPG Industries, Inc., draws glass freely from the surface of the glass melt. There is a submerged clay shape called a draw bar, with bottom flat and top shaped like a blunt cusp, placed vertically below the traction rolls of the drawing machine. This

114

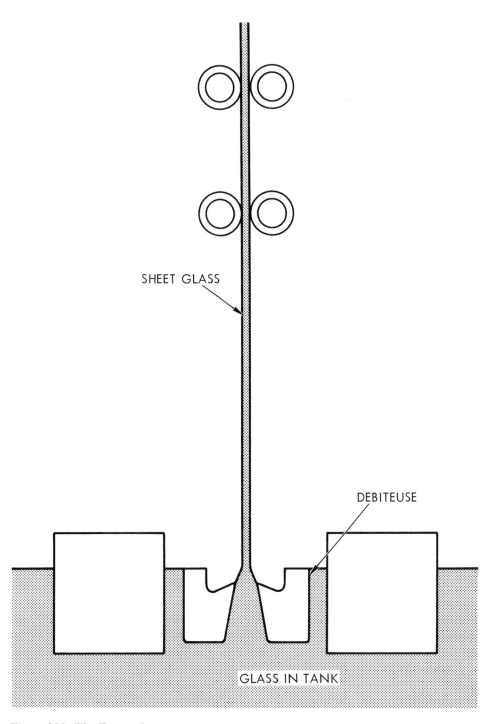

SHEET GLASS

DEBITEUSE

GLASS IN TANK

Figure 111. *The Fourcault process.*

cusp, located several inches below the glass surface, defines the line of draw or generation of the ribbon. As in the Colburn process, the ribbon width is maintained uniform during the first few inches of the draw by cooling the edges. The device used in the Pennvernon is an alloy metal edging device.

As in the Fourcault process, both surfaces are contacted by the drawing rolls.

Corning Microsheet Process

In the Corning Microsheet process, used by the Corning Glass Works, the glass flows downward through a special-shaped refractory die, usually made of platinum. The details of the shape and design of the slot for narrow-width ribbon are suggested in patent 2,880,551. For wider glass, say 14 inches, the details have not been revealed, although the sheet is produced with a bead at the edges for controlling the width.

The glass surface is not contacted by rolls, and the sheet flows downward freely.

Float Glass Process

The float glass process, developed into a commercial success by Pilkington Brothers, Ltd., of England, and used by Libbey-Owens-Ford under license agreement in the United States, takes an endless ribbon of molten glass from the furnace and floats it across the surface of a bath of molten tin. The temperature is lowered as it moves across the tin until it is rigid enough to leave the tin surface and pass through an annealing oven. The glass surfaces are very flat and parallel.

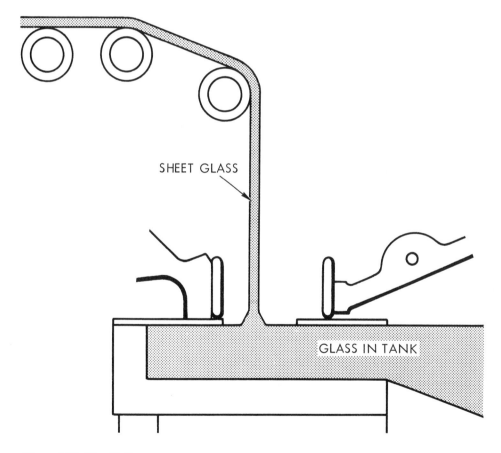

SHEET GLASS

GLASS IN TANK

Figure 112. *The Colburn process.*

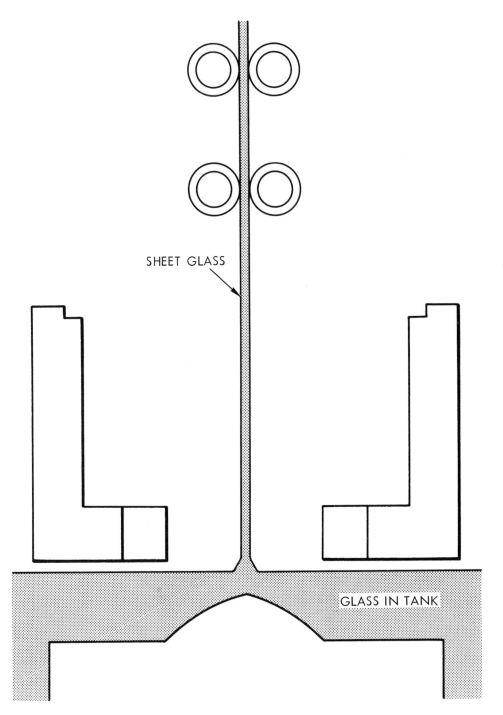

SHEET GLASS

GLASS IN TANK

Figure 113. The Pennvernon process.

Appendices

APPENDIX 1: SOME PHYSICAL PROPERTIES
OF GLASS

1. INTRODUCTION

There are several physical properties important to the artist or craftsman for the control of glass. Glass is a brittle material—everyone is aware of that, even without knowing the scientific definition of brittleness. Glass deforms and flows at high temperature—almost everyone is aware of that. There are expansion-temperature properties, surface-tension properties, and crystallization at high temperatures—few people are aware of these properties. Knowledge of them is important for the successful working of glass, and knowledge of the techniques to measure these properties, like the deformation property, may prove useful. The properties are discussed below.

2. BRITTLENESS

A piece of glass, no matter what its shape—a chunk or bottle or sheet many feet long—is a single material. It is a monolithic piece whereas a stone is an aggregate or polycrystalline material. In glass, a fracture may move or propagate through a piece that is under stress. The fracture may travel an apparently erratic and wandering path with a smooth surface having some irregularities and small waves (see Figure 114).

Under stress, a brittle material deforms a small amount before breaking, while a ductile material deforms a large amount before breaking. As glass is brittle and is of a monolithic nature, it is broken, sawed, ground, scratched, and engraved by a variety of techniques, each designed to control the process and to prevent fracture in the wrong place. For example, glass is sawed with high-speed diamond-impregnated wheels (cutoff saws) which chip out very minute particles.

119

3. Hardness

Glass is a hard material. Of course, "hardness" has many popular meanings: stout, rugged, firm, etc. In technology, hardness can be measured in several different ways. For ceramics and glass, hardness refers to the ability of a material to resist scratching, abrasion, cutting, or penetration. (It should be noted that in the glass industry the terms "hard" or "soft" have special meanings unrelated to this mechanical hardness—they refer to high and low softening temperatures.)

Glasses also vary in mechanical hardness. Resistance to scratching is measured by the scratch hardness test. This test employs an arbitrary hardness scale called the "Mohs scale." It is an ordered scale of several common materials; each material in this group will scratch all materials with a lower hardness number. The materials, in order of increasing hardness, are: 1-talc, 2-gypsum, 3-calcite, 4-fluorite, 5-apatite, 6-orthoclase, 7-quartz, 8-topaz, 9-corundum, and 10-diamond. Glasses lie between apatite and quartz. They vary in hardness depending on their composition. A high lead "crystal" glass can be scratched more easily than a low-expansion borosilicate glass.

Synthetic abrasives have been developed and they are useful for grinding and polishing glass and other materials. The Mohs scale of hardness between orthoclase and diamond has been extended to include garnet, fused zirconia, alumina, silicon carbide, and boron nitride. Alumina and silicon carbide are used for polishing glass.

The simple ordered scale "1-, 2-, 3- . . .10-" has no real working significance. From the point of view of grinding we find that silicon carbide is much more effective than corundum, and diamond very much more effective. When one does actual grinding and lapping tests on glass a scale can be evolved as in Figure 115.

For grinding, we see that silicon carbide is twice as effective as quartz powder, and that diamond is three times as effective as silicon carbide. The hardness of glass may also be observed qualitatively by scratching it with a diamond-point pencil. Differences in glasses will be observed immediately— one can engrave a lead crystal glass much more easily than a borosilicate glass.

4. Flow Deformation

The flow when hot is obviously of prime importance for the glassforming process. Glass becomes less fluid as it cools. The degree of fluidity at a given temperature will depend upon the composition. The composition may vary widely, as is suggested by the three glass compositions given in Section 21 for a lead-oxide glass, a "hard" borosilicate glass, and window glass. The degree of fluidity can be measured experimentally. Thus it is possible to compare different glasses.

Figure 114. *Fracture surfaces of glass.*

5. Fluidity and Temperature

This fluidity, or ease of flow, and its dependence upon temperature, can be made more understandable. Some glasses can be as fluid as No. 20 motor oil when they are heated to 1400–1600°C (2550–2910°F); others might be almost like water in that temperature range. Upon cooling, the glass loses fluidity. At about 800°C (1470°F) the glass may be in a taffy-like state. It will become rigid at a lower temperature, about 450°C (840°F), but not completely rigid, deforming very slowly over many hours.

The effects of these temperatures may be observed in firing a kiln. To correlate with some visual observations, a color-temperature scale may be used:

Degrees Centigrade	Color
600–850	dull red
850–975	cherry red
975–1080	orange
1080–1215	yellow
1215–1270	white
1270–1515	brilliant white

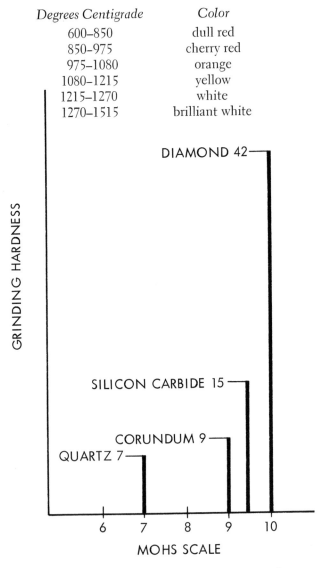

Figure 115. *Relative hardness on a grinding scale.*

It should be noted that glass contains alkalis, and if that alkali is sodium oxide, small amounts volatilized at high temperatures make the flames yellow and may mask the above colors somewhat.

Finally, at a lower temperature than 450°C, glass becomes a rigid and brittle material—the shape made at the higher temperature is now "frozen-in."

6. FLUIDITY AND VISCOSITY

In scientific studies on glass, the term "viscosity" is used rather than "fluidity." Both terms are qualitative and descriptive and have an inverse relationship. That is to say, at high temperatures glass is very fluid—it has a *high* fluidity, but a *low* viscosity; as it cools the glass becomes less fluid—it has a low fluidity and a high viscosity.

7. VISCOSITY COEFFICIENT AND TEMPERATURE

One must make quantitative, experimental measurements on the viscosity of glasses if different ones are to be compared and arranged in some ordered manner. There is a measurable quantity—the coefficient of viscosity—which can be defined, has units, and can be measured over a wide range of temperatures.

No single technique of measurement can be used over the wide range, but three techniques do cover the range with some overlapping. They are: (1) elongation of a vertical, weighted fiber, (2) the sagging of a bar, and (3) the rotating viscometer method, when the glass is quite fluid. The sagging of the bar was discussed in Section 5 and will be discussed further in this section.

8. EXPERIMENTAL RESULTS: THE IMPORTANT "POINTS"

The results of experiments with the above methods can be plotted in the form of a graph (see Figure 116). In practice, however, one concentrates on a few defined "points" of this graph. Three different numerical values of the viscosity coefficient are considered. They are called "strain point viscosity" "annealing point viscosity," and "softening point viscosity." The temperatures which correspond to these values of the viscosity coefficient are presented in commercially prepared tables. The temperatures are called "strain point," "annealing point," and "softening point," in the same way that "freezing point" and "boiling point" are designated. Information which displays such data in tabular form for many glasses may be obtained from the Corning Glass Works, Public Relations Department, Bulletin IZ-1, "Designing with Glass."

The above points are useful in discussing the controlled cooling process, or annealing (see Appendix 2). A fourth viscosity is related to the processes of working glass. This is called the "working point viscosity" and the corresponding temperature is called the "working point." It occurs at a higher temperature than the others and thus at a higher fluidity and a lower viscosity. Glass can be worked in hand-shop operations or machine operations over a range of temperatures about the working point—this is called the "working range." These viscosities are displayed in Figure 116 and the corresponding temperatures can be read off the graph.

Referring to the graph, one has either considerable experimental data so that a smooth curve can be drawn, or the data from the tables so that a smooth curve can be interpolated between the three points. The viscosity is plotted on the vertical scale. It has units, called "poises," which in the centimeter-gram-second system are grams x cm^{-1} x sec^{-1}. The temperature is plotted on the horizontal scale in degrees centrigrade. The temperature scale is linear; the viscosity scale is nonlinear; that is, logarithmic, as one can observe by the numbers going 10^1, 10^2, 10^3, 10^4 . . . alongside the linear markers (see Figure 116). The significance of the viscosity values will be expanded upon in the section "Checking Physical Properties" in this appendix.

Data was obtained from PPG Industries, Inc., L-O-F, and the Corning Glass Works on glasses used for casting or studied for sagging. The three points were plotted and smooth curves were drawn to compare viscosities (see Figure 117).

9. DEVITRIFICATION

This term refers to the growth of crystals within the glass or at the glass surface. This crystal growth may take place at an elevated temperature, close to the working point. As the temperature is increased above this devitrification region, the glass becomes fluid and the crystals dissolve. As the temperature is decreased below this devitrification region the glass is too viscous for growth of crystals. Crystallization takes place more easily at the surface than in the interior and a light crystallization on the surface will make the glass appear frosted. Composition has an important effect on devitrification, some glasses being much more resistant than others. If faced with this problem with a particular glass, it may be simpler to seek out another glass more resistant to crystallization. As sagging and enameling are frequently done at moderately high temperatures so that edges will round over because of surface tension, there is danger of holding the glass in the devitrification range. Experiments will have to be conducted to adjust the heating cycle to minimize this effect. Specific examples of commercial glasses will be considered under "Checking Physical Properties" in this appendix.

10. SURFACE TENSION

The surface-tension property, which is so important for flameworking and glassblowing, giving smooth "fire-polished" surfaces, is of less importance

124

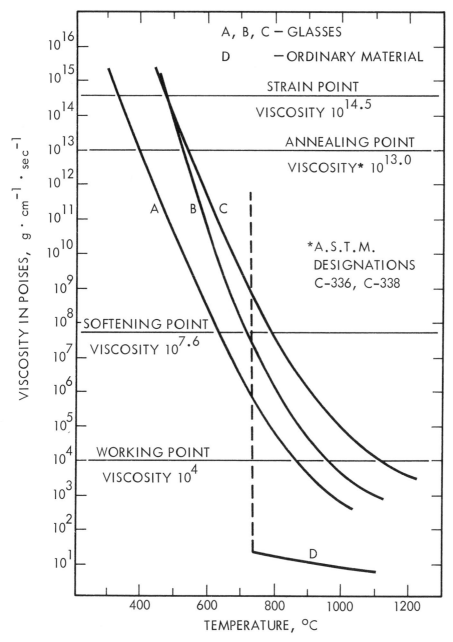

Figure 116. Graph of viscosity coefficient versus temperature for several glasses.

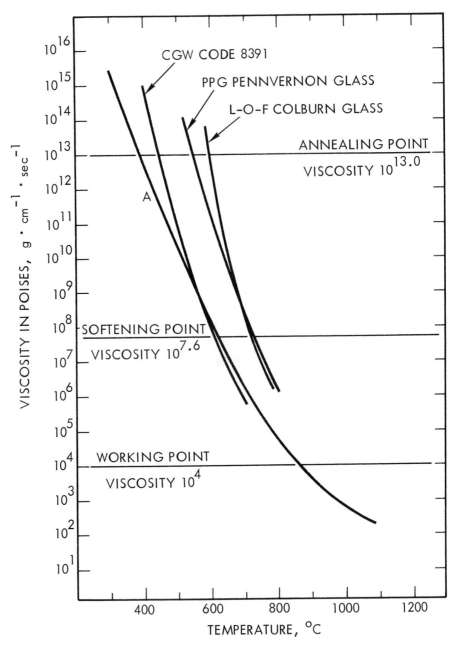

Figure 117. Graph of viscosity coefficient versus temperature for three glasses studied.

for casting. A "free" surface will be smooth; a surface in contact with the mold will be more matte. If one decorates with enamels, which have a lower softening point than does the glass being decorated, then wetting will bond the enamel, and surface tension will smooth it. If one wants to round the edges of the substrate glass, higher temperatures are required to use the surface-tension property of that glass.

11. EXPANSION-TEMPERATURE RELATION

The expansion-temperature relation, commonly called "thermal expansion," is a property of rigid materials, glass included. A piece of rigid material simply changes length with temperature, expanding as the temperature is raised, and contracting as the temperature is lowered. This expansion may vary considerably with glass composition. Fused or glassy silica has a very low expansion, almost zero. As alkali is added to the silica to make a more practical lower-melting batch and lower-softening-point glass, the expansion increases. A low-expansion borosilicate glass has a somewhat higher coefficient of expansion than does the fused silica, and lead-oxide and soda-lime glasses are higher yet. The expansion is given as the change in length, per unit length, per degree centigrade:

$$\alpha \ (\text{expansion coefficient}) = \frac{\dfrac{L - L_o}{L_o}}{{}^{\circ}C}$$

As the change in length, $L - L_o$, is small, the coefficient of expansion is also a small number, as shown below:

Glass	Coefficient of Expansion
Fused Silica	$4 \times 10^{-7} \text{cm/cm/}{}^{\circ}C$
Low-Expansion Borosilicate	$30 \times 10^{-7} \text{cm/cm/}{}^{\circ}C$
Soda-Lime Glass	$85 \times 10^{-7} \text{cm/cm/}{}^{\circ}C$

These would be representative values for the 0-300°C range. These small numbers mean that the change in length over a wide temperature range is still small: A typical soda-lime glass rod, 10 cm. long, will expand only 0.024 cm. on being heated from 0°C to 300°C.

At the low temperature the expansion is usually straight-line, or linear, as shown in Figure 118, but above 300°C it curves up. The 0–300°C range is usually tabulated as a physical property. That could be called the low temperature range value. The high temperature range value, which is from 300°C to the annealing zone, might be three times as large, and is of great importance, but is not usually listed.

127

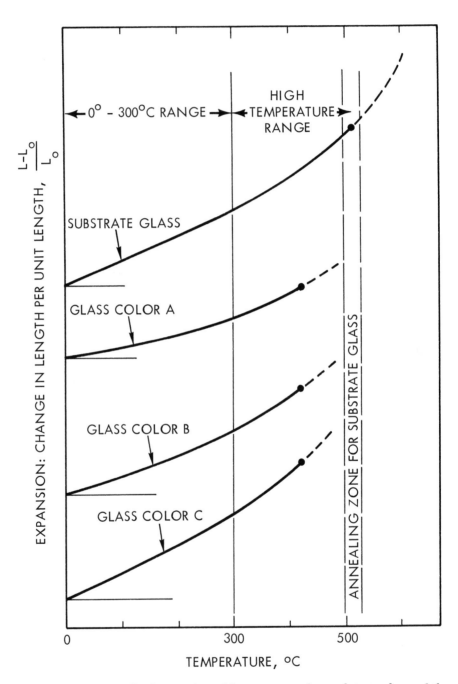

Figure 118. Generalized expansion with temperature for a substrate glass and three glass colors.

12. Working with Different Colors

This expansion-temperature property is extremely important when one combines different colors. Colors might be derived from the same base glass by the addition of small amounts of coloring agents. The expansion-temperature relations may then be changed, and further corrections can be made by the adjustment of the amount of alkali. More alkali will increase the expansion. Thus the colored glass can be adjusted to match the base glass. For glass colors and glass enamels, which are of a different composition than the substrate and have a greatly different softening point, it is important to match the expansion-temperature relation of the enamel to the substrate.

In the graph shown (Figure 119), examples of three different expansion glasses sealed to the surface of a more massive sheet of glass (which has its own coefficient of expansion, the same in all three cases) illustrate how the thin layer can end up (1) in compression, (2) free of stress, or (3) in tension, after cooling. It shows expansion in the 0–300°C range as almost linear or straight-line and that in the 300°C to the sealing temperature range as curving upward. The processing of the glass would be done above the annealing temperature and could approach the softening point for sagging at the same time.

Considering the three examples, the best, of course, is the one free of stress. If the glass on the surface is under compression, it may remain bonded and very strong, like "tempered" glass, unless the compression is excessive; then it may fracture. If the glass on the surface is under tension, it will tend to spall off easily. With increased tension, it may flake off even during the cooling cycle.

13. Checking Physical Properties
Relative Expansion Coefficient

A test for the relative expansion coefficient of two glasses involves sealing the two glasses together, and pulling them out to make a fiber containing the glasses side by side. This fiber, when cool, bends if the expansions are different.

1. Heat two canes, ⅛″ to ⅜″ diameter, in flameworker's torch, one more than the other, but simultaneously.
2. If one is more fluid, apply it to the less fluid and flame off the one that is more fluid (see Figure 120).
3. Heat until both are soft, and pull out a little with tweezers (see Figure 120).
4. Heat narrow region more.
5. Grab end with tweezers, pull out to arm's length, about 24 inches. Do not twist; hold briefly until cool.
6. Snap end section off, and lay against the diagram (see Figure 121), which you must enlarge to full scale.

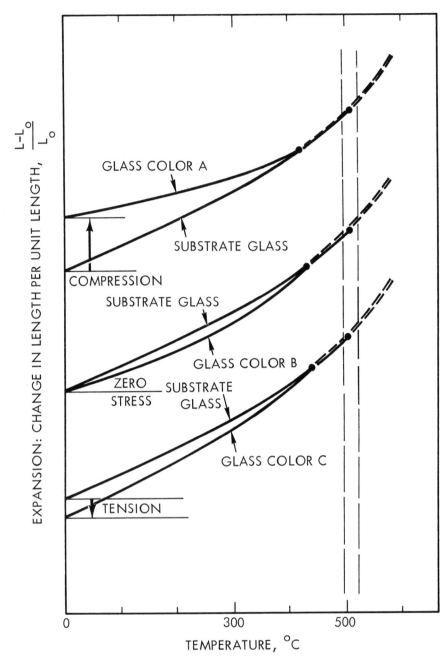

Figure 119. Stress effects of mismatching coefficients of expansion.

Figure 120. Relative expansion test.

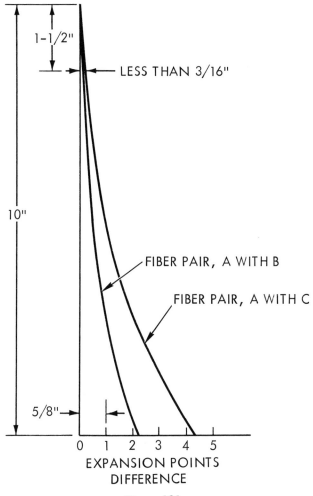

Figure 121.

The difference is measured in "points," with 1 point equal to 1×10^{-7} cm/cm/
°C; more than 5–6 points' difference will give sealing (stress) problems.

Density

Density is mass, or weight, per unit volume. It is determined as mass
density or as weight density. The mass density in the centimeter-gram-second
system would have the units of grams/cm³; the weight density in the British
system would have the units of lbs/ft³.

The density can be determined by weighing an irregularly shaped piece
of glass and then determining or measuring its volume by displacement of
water in a graduated cylinder. From that data one computes density. The
density can be determined by using Archimedes' Principle, weighing the glass
first in air and then submerged in water. The mass density is the ratio of the
mass in air to the difference: (mass in air) - (mass submerged).

131

Devitrification Temperature

The devitrification temperature can be determined neatly by using a "gradient" tube furnace. A ceramic tube, about 1 inch in diameter, and 12 inches long, is wrapped with nichrome or Kanthal heating wire in such a manner that the spacing between loops gradually decreases. Thus one end will run hotter than the other when the whole tube is insulated and power is applied. A thermocouple probe can be used to calibrate position in the tube with temperature. Rods of glass in ceramic boats, placed in the tube furnace, will be exposed to this temperature gradient. The hot end will deform appreciably; at some intermediate place crystals will grow in the glass; the cool end will show no effect. The position above which no crystals form corresponds to the upper devitrification temperature, which may be determined from the calibration curve. Other methods would involve many heating cycles, gradually increasing the maximum temperature, to establish the crystallization conditions.

Softening Point by Sagging

The sagging of a bar of rectangular cross section, held at uniform temperature, was discussed in Section 5. The experimental setup was described there and the equation for the rate of sag was given as:

$$\text{Sagging Rate in Center} = R = \frac{\triangle y}{\triangle t} = K \, \frac{WL^3}{bh^3}$$

with the rate expressed in centimeters of sag per second. The "K" was discussed, and it was pointed out that it varies with temperature and, more precisely, with the viscosity of the glass. That relationship is:

$$K = \frac{1}{19.2\eta}$$

Now we are prepared to expand the discussion of sagging and its relationship to type of glass, shape, and temperature to include the temperature more quantitatively as the coefficient of viscosity. See Figure 122 for the setup of the test bar.

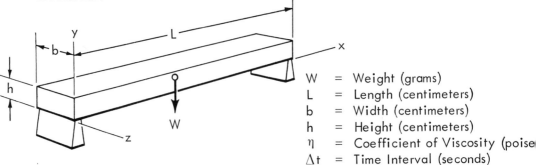

Figure 122. Test bar for measuring sag.

W	=	Weight (grams)
L	=	Length (centimeters)
b	=	Width (centimeters)
h	=	Height (centimeters)
η	=	Coefficient of Viscosity (poise
$\triangle t$	=	Time Interval (seconds)
$\triangle y$	=	Distance of Sag (centimeters)

132

The revised fundamental sagging equation is:

$$\text{Sagging Rate in Center} = R = \frac{\triangle y}{\triangle t} = \frac{WL^3}{19.2\eta bh^3} \text{ (centimeters/second)}$$

$$\text{Distance of Sag in Center} = \triangle y = R \cdot \triangle t \text{ (centimeters)}$$

Suppose we start with some standard dimensions as a basic reference. We then compare thicker glass, like "single strength" window glass with "double strength," or a longer span, or a wider slab. We can build up a table (see Table 8) much like Table 1 in Section 5, but expanded to include viscosity. Briefly, we see that if we increase the temperature so that the viscosity is halved, then we double the rate of sagging. At a temperature close to the softening point, 40°C increase could reduce the viscosity by one-half; 100°C could reduce it to one tenth.

TABLE 8:   SAGGING RATE OF GLASS

	Dimension Effect			Temperature Effect	
	Reference Bar	Double Length Bar	Double Width Bar	Double Thick-ness Bar	Reference Temp.	Reference Temp. +40°C
Length	L	2L	L	L	L	L
Width	b	b	2b	b	b	b
Height	h	h	h	2h	h	h
Weight	W	2W	2W	2W	W	W
Viscosity	η	η	η	η	η	$\frac{1}{2}\eta$

From the above, and by the use of the equation

$$R = \frac{WL^3}{19.2\eta bh^3}, \text{ we calculate}$$

Sagging Rate	R	16R	R	¼R	R	2R

We return to the experimental situation, where we desire now to determine the coefficient of viscosity at a temperature close to the softening point. Let us apply the equation

$$R = \frac{\triangle y}{\triangle t} = \frac{WL^3}{19.2\eta bh^3}$$

to an actual example, namely L-O-F single-strength window glass (thickness, h = 0.30 cm) and thinner "picture glass" (thickness, h = 0.19 cm).

As the properties of this glass are known and tabulated, we can predict some results from the data on viscosity (η versus temperature). The weight can be determined, for a bar of given size, from the density, which is:

$$P = 2.5 \text{ g/cm}^3$$

If we pick:

$$L = 10 \text{ cm}$$
$$b = 1 \text{ cm}$$
$$h = 0.30 \text{ cm}$$

then the volume of the bar is $V = 3 \text{ cm}^3$ and the weight, W, is:

$$W = 7.5 \text{ g}$$

Then:

$$R = \frac{\triangle y}{\triangle t} = \frac{7.5 \text{g} (10 \text{ cm})^3}{19.2 \eta \ (1 \text{ cm}) \ (0.30 \text{ cm})^3}$$

$$= \frac{7.5 \times 1000}{19.2 \eta \times 27 \times 10^{-3}}$$

$$= \frac{1.45 \times 10^4}{\eta}$$

Now we look at the viscosity-temperature data (see Figure 117) and fill in Table 9:

TABLE 9:   RATE OF SAGGING VERSUS TEMPERATURE

Temperature (°C)	Viscosity (g/cm-sec)	$Rate = R = \dfrac{\triangle y \ cm}{\triangle t \ sec}$
710°	10^7	1.45 cm/1000 sec
810°	10^6	1.45 cm/100 sec
880°	10^5	1.45 cm/10 sec
930°	10^4	1.45 cm/1 sec

We experimented with:

Bar A	Bar B
L = 10 cm	L = 10 cm
b = 1.1 cm	b = 1.0 cm
h = 0.30 cm	h = 0.19 cm

held at 650°C for 12 minutes, or 720 seconds. The distance of sag was 0.7 cm. and 1.5 cm., respectively. The bars weighed 8.8 g and 5.0 g respectively.

We solve the equation for η, substitute the above experimental values, and determine that:

$$\eta = \frac{1}{R} \frac{WL^3}{19.2 \ bh^3}$$

Bar A = $\eta = 3.0 \times 10^8$ at 650°C
Bar B = $\eta = 3.5 \times 10^8$ at 650°C

This is good agreement, considering how crude the experiment is, and it agrees well with the tabulated viscosity. We now see how this technique can be used to study sagging processing temperatures, or viscosity.

We then applied this technique to seven different colored glasses made by the Kokomo Opalescent Glass Company. These were sheet glass, so strips were cut off with the wheel cutter, and dimensions were measured. The thicknesses were not the same, and thus the previous analysis showing how thickness enters into sagging was pertinent. After measurement and analysis of the data, it became immediately obvious that the viscosity-temperature curves of these glasses were not the same (they fell into three groups). This meant that the annealing temperatures were not the same. Further, we were alerted that other physical properties might be different also—coefficient of expansion, for example. We conclude that all glasses from a manufacturer have to be checked before use, when the intention is to combine them.

Deformation Rate by Sagging

Once one recognizes that the softening point does change with composition changes, then one may use the sagging method to study different colored glasses. If these glasses are produced in a reliable manner, once studies are done the results will be valid indefinitely. On the other hand, if there is a suspicion of variable properties, the sagging method can be used as a check on reliability. Test bars will give data that can be interpreted for other dimensions. As the dimensions are changed the rate will change, as was shown by the analysis and Table 8, and by the data on the L-O-F window glass and the thinner "picture" glass. One can then predict from the test bar results how long it will take another shape to sag at a given temperature; one can predict which way to shift the temperature and, roughly, how far to shift it to change the rate a given amount.

Casting Viscosity

Experiments with casting Corning Glass Works Code 8391 glass and L-O-F window glass show that casting viscosity is in the range near working-point viscosity, which was what we expected.

Summary of Studies

The summary of the studies on L-O-F window glass for sagging, wetting and sealing, surface tension rounding off, casting, and devitrification is presented in Figure 123. These results are superimposed on the viscosity curve.

Summary of Tests on Commercial Glasses

We compared several glasses for devitrification in the casting range. No imported glasses were considered, for the suppliers would furnish no data on physical properties. The glasses tested were the Corning Glass Works Code 8391 glass, ten from the Blenko Glass Company, ten from the Kokomo Opalescent Glass Company, four from the Paul Wissmach Glass Company, and the L-O-F window glass.

135

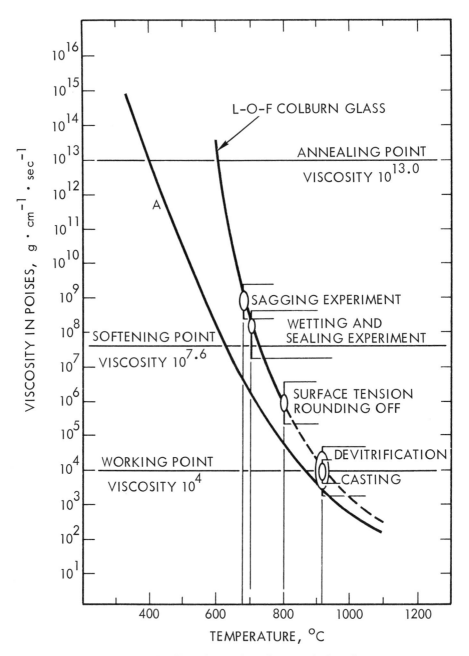

Figure 123. *Experimental studies on window glass.*

These glasses show slight differences in temperatures for casting. The CGW and Blenko glasses show no devitrification; the Kokomo glasses show considerable, as does the window glass, and the Paul Wissmach glasses show excessive devitrification.

We recommend the Blenko glasses for general work in glassforming techniques; the Kokomo glasses should be adequate for sagging and enameling and are more uniform in sheet thickness than the Blenko glasses; we do not recommend other glasses or imported glasses. The Corning Glass Works 8391 would be an ideal clear composition, but is an optical glass, expensive and not ordinarily available.

14. Use of "Soft" and "Hard" (Borosilicate) Glasses

The lower working temperature lead-oxide glass (or soda-lime glass) is Called a "soft" glass, while the higher working temperature borosilicate glass is called a 'hard' glass. The use of the hard glass is restricted to flameworking techniques, which require temperatures that can be easily attained in the propane-oxygen flame. For casting, the desired degree of fluidity must be attained at reasonable temperatures, so that a relatively inexpensive electrical furnace can be made. The upper temperature of operation is then 1000°C. As noted before, the Corning Glass Works glass could be cast at about 860°C, and the Kokomo and Blenko glasses around 900°C. L-O-F window glass would require more like 1000°C.

The soft glass has a high expansion, and although it can be cooled quickly from the casting temperature to the annealing temperature, it must be cooled gradually below that temperature or it will crack (see Appendix 2, on annealing).

An important reason for using the soft glass is that a wide range of colors is available commercially, or, if the craftsman wants to experiment with making colored glass, colors can be made by remelting cullet with oxides in fireclay crucibles, using a gas-fired pottery kiln, at reasonable temperatures. Colors in the hard glass are limited in commercial availability, and are more difficult to make, requiring appreciably higher melting temperatures.

APPENDIX 2: ANNEALING PROCEDURES AND HEATING CYCLES

15. General Remarks

If glass is cooled quickly to room temperature following the glassforming process at elevated temperatures, the piece will be subject to high stresses and may crack. If no crack forms immediately, the piece will be very sensitive to slight additional stress and a crack may form after a while. The sensitivity to fracture can be reduced with a proper cooling treatment, which minimizes the stress in the glass. This proper cooling treatment is called annealing.

One may contrast the glassforming processes with flameworking, not only for design and technique, which have been discussed in various sections, but also as regards the crucial cooling step. Flameworking uses low expansion borosilicate glass of small size or moderate thickness, and annealing is not difficult to achieve. Laminating, sagging, fusing, and casting use a relatively high expansion glass, with some mismatch of expansion of different colors, and the designs tend to be massive in area. So for the glassforming processes the cooling step is much more critical and an annealing furnace with some kind of temperature control is desired.

Annealing was known in ancient times to be an important step in glassmaking. Theophilus, of about A.D. 1140, who was mentioned in Section 3, described in *The Various Arts*, Book II, Chapter II, *"The Annealing Kiln,"* how objects are put into "the annealing kiln, which should be moderately heated." Once again we recommend this book on diverse arts, including glassmaking, as a most interesting historical document on the crafts and craftsmanship.

16. Principles of Annealing

During annealing the glass is held or "soaked" at an elevated temperature (the annealing point temperature, described in Appendix 1) for about 20 minutes and then cooled slowly. It is soaked to permit all of the glass to come to the annealing temperature. As previously mentioned, the furnace in which this is done commercially is called a lehr. If the design is of a "continuous" type, the glass is carried through on an endless metal chain belt. The craftsman will be interested in a more modest annealing furnace of a batch type, as that is much less expensive.

If the same furnace is used for glassforming as for annealing, then the temperature is decreased from the processing temperature to the annealing temperature, the glass is soaked and then cooled. If the glass is formed outside of the annealing furnace, for example by flameworking or glassblowing, upon completion the object is placed in the annealing furnace, soaked and cooled. If the temperature of the object has dropped below the annealing point, then the object must be heated first and soaked.

17. TEMPERATURE-TIME CYCLES FOR ANNEALING

The complete annealing process may be looked at as a heating step, which must not be so rapid as to break the object; a soaking step, which will relieve stresses introduced by the heating; a cooling step from the high temperature region to about 75°C below the annealing point; and a cooling step from there to room temperature. Both of the cooling steps are to be slow enough that stress can be partially relieved and not become too great. The overall temperature-time cycle is shown in Figure 124.

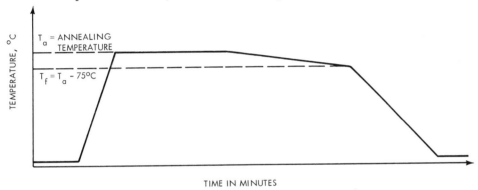

Figure 124. Generalized temperature-time cycle for annealing.

There is a formula for the heating rate and cooling rate. This formula is discussed in detail in *Flameworking* by Frederic Schuler. A particular example of the use of the tables in *Flameworking* is as follows:

1. Soft glass
2. The annealing temperature is found to be $T_a = 500°C$.
3. Therefore, $T_a - 75°C = T_f = 425°C$
4. Consider that the piece is 1 inch thick.
5. The cooling and heating rates are found in the tables:
$$R_h = 13°C/\text{minute}$$
$$R^* = 1.1°C/\text{minute}$$
$$R_f = 9°C/\text{minute}$$
6. The time of heating, t_h, from room temperature, which is about 20°C, to the annealing temperature, $T_a = 500°C$, at the heating rate, $R_h = 13°C/\text{minute}$; the time of cooling, t^*, from $T_a = 500°C$ to $T_a - 75°C = 425°C$, at $R^* = 1.1°C/\text{minute}$; and finally, the time of cooling, t_f, from T_f to room temperature at $R_f = 9°C/\text{minute}$, are given by:

139

$$t_h = \frac{480°C}{13°C/min} = 37 \text{ minutes}$$

$$t^* = \frac{75°C}{1.10C/min} = 67 \text{ minutes}$$

$$t_f = \frac{405°C}{9°C/min} = 45 \text{ minutes}$$

The graph looks like this (see Figure 125):

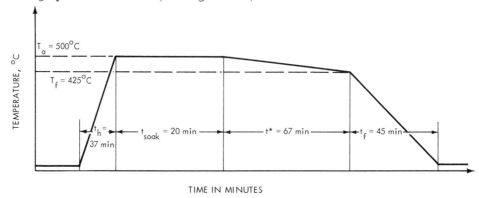

TIME IN MINUTES

Figure 125. *Annealing cycle for a particular example.*

18. Temperature-Time Cycles for Casting, Fusing, Sagging, and Enameling, Followed by Annealing

Now we consider the overall processing cycle, which should even include drying the molds. The cycles all have features in common—namely, to increase the temperature to that desired for carrying out the process, hold there briefly, decrease to the annealing temperature, hold there to soak—to bring the piece to a uniform temperature—then decrease slowly in the high temperature cooling region, and finally more rapidly to room temperature.

The upper temperature for each process varies for a given composition (that is, for a given viscosity-temperature relation) although longer times can be equivalent to increasing the temperature. The dimensions affect the processing conditions, shown clearly in the case of sagging, as was discussed in Section 5 and Appendix 1. The differing of viscosity-temperature relations with composition was described in Appendix 1 also.

The general processing cycle is illustrated in Figure 126.

Now we would like to consider some of the processes in detail: drying, casting (or fusing, or sagging and enameling), and finally annealing.

For drying the plaster-sand molds, we like to let the mold air-dry for several days, after measuring the volume of glass required, and then start the processing cycle. These molds would be used for casting or fusing, and can be used for sagging. (If the bisque-fired terra-cotta is used for sagging, then there is no drying cycle.) The molds containing the glass are slowly heated to 100°C with the furnace door open, held at 100°C for several hours, and heated slowly to 300°C (see Figure 127). (Note: Hydroperm has an organic

140

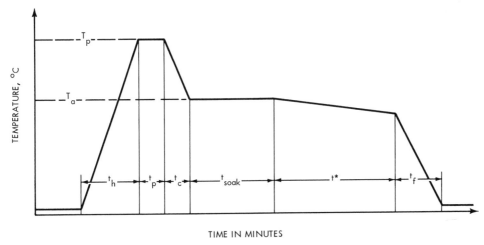

Figure 126. *Generalized processing cycle for glassforming processes.*

additive which burns out by 300°C.) It may be convenient to do this part overnight.

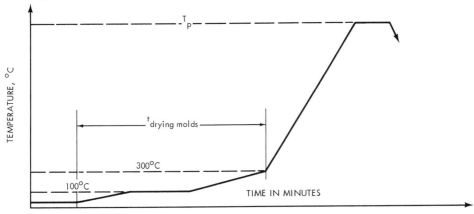

Figure 127.

The furnace lid or door is closed, the control turned to high heat, and the processing cycle continued, until the processing temperature is reached. This processing, for casting, is shown in Figure 128, which represents a con-

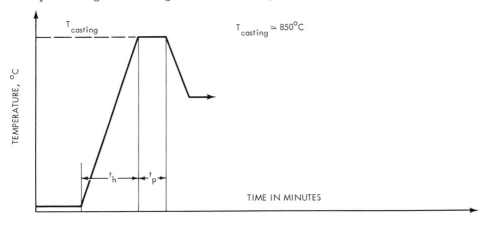

Figure 128.

141

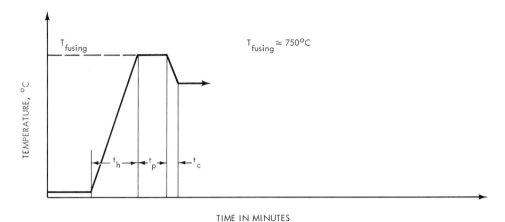

Figure 129.

tinuation of the drying cycle. The casting temperature is about 850°C. Several remarks can be made: First, the casting temperature depends on the glass properties. For example, the Corning Glass Works Code 8391 glass is clearly less viscous at 800°C than is the Blenko glass. Second, the surface quality is altered by the processing conditions. Overfiring (50°C will make an appreciable difference) causes the surface in contact with the mold to become much more matte and to lose the satiny finish with its considerable sheen.

The figures shown for the different processes can actually serve as work sheets, or photocopies can be pasted in a notebook for studying different glasses and for recording data.

The fusing temperature is indicated as being about 750°C in Figure 129. It is clear that the amount of flow is much less than for casting, and the process is intermediate between casting and laminating.

The sagging temperature is indicated as being about 700°C in Figure 130. The processing is complicated by laminating or sealing several glasses

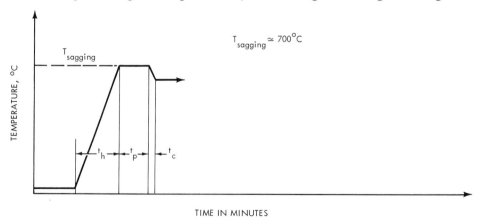

Figure 130.

142

together, by enameling, and by the desire to round off edges of the glass by using surface tension. Sagging itself could be done at lower temperatures, and the rounding off might require somewhat higher temperatures. These processes were considered in the studies presented in Appendix 1. It should be remembered that the glass composition (viscosity-temperature) has its effect on the sagging temperature.

Each of the processes is continued by cooling to the annealing temperature and then by annealing, as shown in Figure 131. Finally, the mold and glass reach room temperature and can be safely removed from the furnace for further handling.

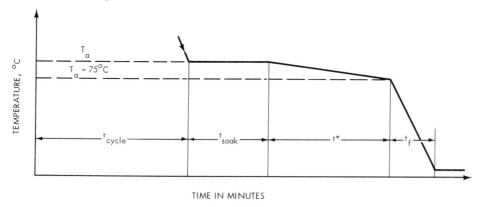

Figure 131.

19. Testing for Stress by Using Polarized Light

All the discussion of reducing stress in glass by (1) matching coefficients of expansion when different glasses are used and (2) proper annealing does not lead to a feeling of confidence unless there is a test to tell you if the processing has been done correctly. That is, the glass might have a high level of stress and not break for days or months. However, if the stress level is really low, then the glass will never break from stress.

Therefore, we need to observe the level of stress by using polarized light. The object is placed between two sheets of polarizing acetate plastic, say 10" x 10" each, with a light source behind the second sheet. If the object is viewed through the first sheet, stressed areas appear to have bands of light and dark. The two polarizing sheets can be turned so that maximum light is transmitted, and then there will be dark bands, or so that minimum light is transmitted, and then there will be light bands. The number of bands increases with increased stress; comparison with some commercial objects of low stress will enable one to identify a desirable low-stress pattern.

APPENDIX 3: REFERENCES

1—R. W. Smith, *Glass from the Ancient World: The Ray Winfield Smith Collection*, The Corning Museum of Glass, Corning, N.Y., 1957

2—J. D. Cooney, "Glass Sculpture in Ancient Egypt," *Journal of Glass Studies*, II:11, 1960

3—F. Schuler, "Ancient Glassmaking Techniques: The Egyptian Core Vessel Process," *Archaeology* 15:32 (Spring) 1962

4—D. Labino, "The Egyptian Sand-Core Technique: A New Interpretation," *Journal of Glass Studies* VIII: 124, 1966

5—F. Schuler, "Ancient Glassmaking Techniques: The Molding Process," *Archaeology* 12:47 (Spring) 1959

6—F. Schuler, "Ancient Glassmaking Techniques: Egyptian Fused Miniature Mosaics," *Advances in Glass Technology*, Part 2, 206, New York, 1963

7—F. Schuler, "Ancient Glassmaking Techniques: The Blowing Process," *Archaeology* 12:116 (Summer) 1959

8—R. J. Charleston, "Some Tools of the Glassmaker in Medieval and Renaissance Times, with Special Reference to the Glassmaker's Chair," *Glass Technology*, III, No. 3:107 (June) 1962

APPENDIX 4: LIST OF SUPPLIERS

Abrasives

Norton Company
Worcester, Massachusetts 01606

Acid, Hydrofluoric

Allied Chemical
Industrial Chemicals Division
P.O. Box 70
Morristown, New Jersey 07960

E. I. Du Pont de Nemours & Co.
Inc.
Industrial and Biochemical Department
Wilmington, Delaware 19898

The Harshaw Chemical Company
1945 East 97th Street
Cleveland, Ohio 44106

Diamond Points

Anton Smith and Co., Inc.
111 Eighth Avenue
New York, New York

Epoxies

Furane
5121 San Fernando Road, West
Los Angeles, California 90039

Flameworking Accessories

Bethlehem Apparatus Company,
Inc.
Hellertown, Pennsylvania

Eisler Engineering Co.
740-770 South 13th Street
Newark, New Jersey

Flameworking Torches

Bethlehem Apparatus Co., Inc.
Hellertown, Pennsylvania

Eisler Engineering Co.
740-770 South 13th Street
Newark, New Jersey

National Welding Equipment
Division of Veriflo Corporation
835 National Court
Richmond, California

Glass, Sheet, Colored

S. A. Bendheim Co., Inc.
122 Hudson Street
New York, New York 10013
(handles Kokomo glass)

Blenko Glass Company
Milton, West Virginia 25541

Kokomo Opalescent Glass Company
P.O. Box 809
Kokomo, Indiana 46901

Leo Popper and Sons
143 Franklin Street
New York, New York
(importer)

The Paul Wissmach Glass Company, Inc.
420 Stephens Street
Paden City, West Virginia 26159

Glass, Sheet, Window

(Contact your nearest dealer)

American St. Gobain Corp.
P.O. Box 929
Kingsport, Tenn. 37662

Libbey-Owens-Ford Company
Technical Sales Services and
Public Relations Department
811 Madison Avenue
Toledo, Ohio 43624

PPG Industries Inc.
Public Relations
One Gateway Center
Pittsburgh, Pennsylvania 15222

Glass, Rod, Colored
Conlon Glass Associates, Inc.
10 Bethpage Road
Hicksville, New York 11802

Glass, Rod and Tubing, Clear
(Order through your nearest
dealer)
Corning Glass Works
(Borosilicate glass and soft or
"flint" glass)

Kimble Laboratory Glassware
Owens-Illinois Glass Company
(Borosilicate glass and soft or
"flint" glass)

Glass, Cullet or Chunk, Colored
Blenko Glass Company
Milton, West Virginia 25541

Glass Colors and Glass Enamels
Ceramic Color and Chemical Mfg. Co.
P.O. Box 297
New Brighton, Pennsylvania 15066

Drakenfeld Division
Imperial Color and Chemical De-
partment
Hercules Incorporated
Washington, Pennsylvania 15301

Ferro Corporation
60 Greenway Drive
Pittsburgh, Pennsylvania 15204

The Harshaw Chemical Company
Division of Kawanee Oil Co.
1945 East 97th Street
Cleveland, Ohio 44106

Pemco Division
The Glidden Company
5601 Eastern Avenue
Baltimore, Maryland 21224

Glassforming and Annealing Furnaces
Electric
A. D. Alpine Inc.
353 Coral Circle
El Segundo, California 90245

Cress Electric Furnaces
Recco Equipment Company
323 West Maple Avenue
Monrovia, California 91016

Gas
A. D. Alpine, Inc.
353 Coral Circle
El Segundo, California 90245

Grinding Wheels (Mills and Laps),
Belt Sanders, Polishing Equipment,
Steel and Tungsten-Carbide Glass
Cutters
Somaca-Western
852 Aldo Avenue
Santa Clara, California 95050

Sommer and Maca
Glass Machinery Company
5501 West Ogden Avenue
Chicago, Illinois 60650

Plaster
(Any building or ceramic sup-
ply house)
United States Gypsum Company
101 South Wacker Drive
Chicago, Illinois 60606

Polarizing Plastic Sheet
Edmund Scientific Co.
801 Edscorp Building
Barrington, New Jersey 08007

Saws, Diamond, Cutoff
Felker Manufacturing Company
1128 Border Avenue
Torrance, California 90501

Silica (Sand)
(Any ceramic supply house)
Waxes
Dick Ells Co.
908 Venice Boulevard
Los Angeles, California 90015

146

APPENDIX 5: BIBLIOGRAPHY

Anderson, D. M.: *The Art of Written Forms*, Holt, Rinehart and Winston, New York, 1969

Dodwell, C. R.: *Theophilus: De Diversis Artibus*, Thomas Nelson and Sons, Ltd., London, 1961

Eliscu, F.: *Sculpture in Clay, Wax and Slate*, Chilton Book Co., Philadelphia, 1959

Hoover, H. C. and Hoover, L. H.: *Agricola: De Re Metallica (1556)*, Dover Publications, Inc., New York, 1950

Kinney, K.: *Glass Craft*, Chilton Book Co., Philadelphia, 1962

Knoblaugh, R. R.: *Modelmaking for Industrial Design*, McGraw-Hill Book Co., New York, 1958

Koch, R.: *The Book of Signs*, Dover Publications, Inc., New York

Norton, F. H.: *Ceramics for the Artist Potter*, Addison-Wesley Publishing Co., Inc., Cambridge, Mass., 1956

Panofsky, E.: *On the Abbey Church of St. Denis and its Art Treasures*, Princeton, 1946

Phillips, C. J.: *Glass, the Miracle Maker*, Pitman Publishing Corp., New York, 1946

Reyntien, P.: *The Technique of Stained Glass*, Watson-Guptill Publications, New York, 1967

Rhodes, D.: *Clay and Glazes for the Potter*, Chilton Book Co., Philadelphia, 1957

Röttger, E. and Klante, D.: *Creative Drawing*, Reinhold Book Corporation, New York, 1963

Schuler, F.: *Flameworking: Glassmaking for the Craftsman*, Chilton Book Co., Philadelphia, 1968

Vasari, G.: *On Technique*, Dover Publications, Inc., New York, 1960

Warner, L.: *The Enduring Art of Japan*, Harvard University Press, Cambridge, 1952

Weyl, W. A.: *Coloured Glasses*, The Society of Glass Technology, Sheffield, 1951

Williams, E. (editor): *An Anthology of Concrete Poetry*, Something Else Press, New York, 1967

Index

About the Authors

FREDERIC W. SCHULER was born in Monroe, Wisconsin, and received his Ph.D. in physical chemistry from the University of Wisconsin in 1949. He has worked in industrial research and development in the areas of vacuum-deposited thin films, glass chemistry, and electrochemical batteries. He is teaching physics and engineering, including graphics, at Santa Barbara City College, Santa Barbara, California.

He has long been interested in glassmaking techniques and has worked, or is working actively now, in flameworking, casting, and free-blowing. From 1956 to 1958 he was administrator of the Scientific Research Program, Corning Museum of Glass, Corning, New York. For three years previous to that he was senior research associate of the Fundamental Chemistry Group at the Corning Glass Works. He met Frederick Carder, founder of Steuben Glass, while associated with the Corning Museum of Glass and had a chance to work on casting methods in Mr. Carder's workshop. He has been interested in the studies of ancient technologies, with emphasis on tools and techniques, and has published several articles on ancient glassmaking techniques. He also wrote: *Flameworking, Glassmaking for the Craftsman* (Chilton Book Company, Philadelphia, 1968).

His outside activities now lie mainly in the field of sculpture, although earlier he worked in lithography and watercolor painting. He studied for five years with the sculptor Stanislaus Szukalski. He now works by himself, at present mainly in clay and plaster. He is especially interested in the design of alphabets and calligraphy and is experimenting with casting calligraphic reliefs in glass.

Dr. Schuler, his wife, and four children now live in Santa Barbara.

LILLI SCHULER was born in Italy and lived there, and in Switzerland, Argentina, and England. She comes from an artistic family: One brother, Oscar Bucher, is a craft potter in Santa Barbara and the other, Otmar Bucher, is a graphic designer in Zürich, Switzerland.

She became interested in glassmaking techniques when she married Dr. Frederic Schuler, and moved to Corning, New York. At that time her husband was working in photosensitive glass, which had interesting architectural and design potential. She followed the progress of this work and also was excited by the glassblowers and engravers of the Steuben Glass factory.

After moving to Santa Barbara, she helped her husband with his studies on ancient casting techniques. She also worked with him on flameworking techniques and has continued to experiment with her own designs and methods. In a similar manner, she has been working with her husband on glassforming techniques.